TO HEAR THEM TELL IT

Memories of Growing Up in Charleston

Compiled by

MARY C. COY

CHARLESTON GUIDE BOOKS
PUBLISHING COMPANY

Published by Charleston Guide Books
Charleston, SC
www.charlestonguidebooks.com

Notice: The information in this book is true and complete to the best of our knowledge. It is offered without guarantee on the part of the author or publisher. The author disclaims all liability in connection with the use of this book.

ISBN-10: 0985152656
ISBN-13: 9780985152659

Manufactured in the United States of America

DEDICATION

This book is dedicated to all of the wonderful people who were interviewed for this project. Without their interest, time and patience, it would not have been possible. The book is also a tribute to my relatives, living and dead, who taught me an appreciation of the city, its people and their customs.

TABLE OF CONTENTS

Growing Up in the 1940s and 50s

ACKNOWLEDGEMENTS

Sincere thanks to Laura Donnelly, Pam Gabriel, Katherine Clark, and Diane Owens for sharing their suggestions and skills in editing;

to Derrick Kinloch for creating a visual representation of locations described in this book;

and to Jack Duane, Pam Gabriel and Claire Robinson for first sparking the idea for this project.

INTRODUCTION

As a native Charlestonian, I am often asked by newcomers and visitors what the city was like when I was growing up. That's a topic most of us over the age of fifty love talking about! Not only do we enjoy regaling newcomers with our stories, we love it even more when we're in the company of other Charlestonians and can compare notes, asking each other, "Hey, do you remember ...?" It's human nature to reflect on the passing years, and for Charlestonians, it is a particularly poignant subject. Our city has morphed over the last several decades from a quiet, economically-deprived community to one of the most exciting and desirable places to live. We are proud of the aesthetic, economic and societal strides the city has made, but we also find it important to let others know how things used to be. Even though the "good old days" weren't always good, they weren't all bad either.

In the pages of this book, you will glimpse a picture of Charleston that's been painted through the eyes of men and women who grew up here. The image is drawn from my interviews of over two dozen Charlestonians whose recollections typify those of many residents of a time now faded. Included in this collection are people who came from well-to-do families as well as those who grew up less fortunate - Charlestonians from nearly every section of the city, both uptown and downtown. You will occasionally find common memories which serve as threads that tie the stories together. Those of us who grew up here will remember and relate to much of what they have to say. In fact, most readers of this anthology will likely be native Charlestonians who want to take a stroll down memory lane.

But for those readers who are "from off," these stories might amuse and enlighten. Charlestonians have always known that we have something special here, and now others have come to discover this for themselves. Even when Charleston looked like "an unpainted village," as my uncle used to call it, we still knew the city had charm. Looks didn't seem to matter, and as in the old adage, it is what's inside that counts anyway. What was inside were the people. They are the cogs of the wheel that made this city spin.

Old Charleston is barely recognizable amidst today's spit and polish. Our buildings, culture, customs, language and cuisine have all changed. There is a new Charleston now – one that is more colorful, vibrant and trendy.

One thing about being native Charlestonians is that we've been able to experience the best – and sometimes the worst - of both worlds. So come with us and hear the stories of what it was like to grow up in Charleston during the first half of the 20th century.

KEY

1 - Walter V. Duane

2 - Clementa Iamundo Florio

3 - George Breibart

4 - Buddy Bendt

5 - Inez Spalviero Cox

6 - Rutledge Cox

7 - Betty Ravenel Hennessy

8 - Lewis Bowen

9 - Ginny Blank Bowen

10 - Ralph McLaughlin

11 - Rosie Phillips Dursse

12 - Jeanne Moseley Jeffcoat

13 - Creighton Hay

14 - Marty Moseley

15 - Arthur (Skipper) Jenkins, Jr.

16 - Dan Croghan

17 - Spero Drake

18 - Frederick Stuhr

19 - Rosemary (Binky) Read Cohen

20 - Gaillard Dotterer

21 - Missy Siegling Blocker

22 - Phyllis Dawson Moseley

23 - Sondra Pfaehler

24 - Sue Schwerin Veon

25 - Martin Lazarus

Ashley
River

Cooper
River

Points on this map are approximate locations.

A BOROUGH BOY

Walter V. Duane

Walter Duane can tell you just about anything you want to know about Charleston - who, what, where, when, how and why – because he's witnessed most of it first-hand over the past ninety-plus years. And what he didn't experience, his parents told him about. So he also has their tales stored in his memory bank.

Walter was a 'borough boy' and grew up at 16 Wall Street. That area of Ansonborough was leveled in 1965 to make way for the Gaillard Municipal Auditorium. Walter says that Ansonborough was a 'checkerboard' neighborhood, one that was racially mixed. "Ansonborough was primarily white working class families, but there were no segregated neighborhoods in Charleston. Some were predominately white or black, but there were no laws out-lawing blacks from living on Tradd Street, Elliott Street, Wall Street or any other streets. The Catholic church for black people (St. Peter's) was in Ansonborough, on Wentworth Street between Anson and Meeting, but some whites went there because it was close to where they lived. The back yard of the church backed up to the convent for the black Oblate Sisters of Providence who taught at a black Catholic school (St. Peter's) which was also in Ansonborough - on Society Street."

The black family next door to Walter's "lived there the entire time we lived there. They went to the big (Emmanuel AME) church on Calhoun Street. They owned their house and lived upstairs; they rented the bottom out to different black people over the years, including blacksmith Philip Simmons. The family included a niece

1

and her husband who had a job as a porter on the railroad. I think he worked in the dining car because we'd see him coming and going with a white coat on. He was a nice man – and very dignified. After he died, she married again. Her second husband was a chef at the Francis Marion Hotel."

Walter explains, "Charleston was not a segregated city until after the Second World War. Black people lived on nearly every street. Sometime they lived in the back yard in a carriage house which they usually rented from whites. When I was a kid, Rainbow Row was an integrated area but was mainly black families. A white man who worked with me at the phone company in the 1970s bragged about how he was living 'below Broad' on Elliott Street which runs right next to Rainbow Row. So I called a black co-worker over to the desk and asked him, 'How many black families are on Elliott Street these days?' and he said one. Then I said to him, 'Didn't you used to live there?' and he said yes. So I said, 'How many white families lived there when you did?' and he said one. I then said to both men, 'Meet your neighbor.'"

By 1950, Walter says that a lot of white people were moving to the sub-urbs or uptown around Hampton Park. "They wanted new houses. People wanted to modernize. Old houses were more costly to heat than newer ones. And the government would loan money to build new homes but not to fix up old ones. The population of the city dropped so much that supposedly they wouldn't even say what it was because it was so small compared to what it had been. All over the country, cities were losing people. And not only would they lose the taxes but they lost people who could help the cities. That is when Mayor Palmer Gaillard starting annexing some areas across the Ashley. In the late 1950s, there was somewhat of a trend to move back to the cities, but it was a much slower trend than when people had moved out.

"Our church, old St. Joseph's Catholic Church on Anson Street, was closed in the mid-60s because there were so few members left. It had been a great neighborhood when we were kids, but Ansonborough was running down. There were beer parlors on Calhoun Street and it became a rough area. We always felt that Ansonborough was the best part of town, but very little was done to preserve it. In 1958, they started talking about preserving some of the neighborhood, but most of the old families had already moved. Some of us would never have moved otherwise. The city finally decided to put the municipal auditorium there, and that's when Wall Street was demolished."

The church was a big part of neighborhood life in 'the borough.' Walter says, "On Christmas Eve, most families in our area went to Midnight Mass at St. Joseph's, so hundreds of people would be walking the street. As you were going there, you would see doors opening all along the way."

The church is now St. John's Reformed Episcopal Church and is home to the Philip Simmons Garden which pays tribute to the icon of Charleston's ironwork. "The church was built before the Civil War as a Presbyterian chapel for slaves. Then during the Civil War, it became a Catholic church. The Irish Volunteers attended Mass there just before they set off to fight at Bull Run. Then a hundred years later, the African-American congregation that now owns it purchased it from the Catholic Diocese. It is a beautiful little church."

Walter attended St. Joseph's parochial school. The large school bell is still in the yard near the corner of Anson and George Streets. The school building now serves as the church hall for the current congregation. "We had four classrooms in the school - two big ones and two small ones. One of the small ones was first grade. The second and third grades were in one room, and fourth and fifth in another. Sixth was by itself. First graders were sent home from school every day about noon, and the others at around two o'clock. Most of the kids lived in the neighborhood so they walked home. It was safe and there was not much traffic."

Walter at 16 Wall Street

Walter says, "In those days we'd walk anywhere. You'd see other people on the street and run into somebody you knew going the same direction. We used to hear that people in New York didn't know their neighbors, but everyone in Charleston knew everyone else – or were related. Kids walked to school, and adults would walk to work and almost anywhere on the peninsula. We'd occasionally walk to Hampton Park which was over twenty blocks from our neighborhood. There was a streetcar, but most of the time, people walked. Sometime mothers would tell kids to go ride the bus on a Sunday just to get them out of the house, but very few people rode the bus or drove on a regular basis."

In the evenings, even after dark, "older people would sit on their doorsteps. Kids played in the streets - games like 'Fox and geese and they all fly over,' and 'Take baby steps and giant steps.' We'd go down to the Seaboard railroad lot where Harris Teeter is now and play ball. For a while, a boy whose daddy was a fireman lived next door to us, and we'd go over to the fire station on Wentworth and Meeting. In those days, they still had a few horses to pull the fire engines, so they had a lot of sawdust there for the horses. We'd get in the garage and jump down from the roof into the sawdust. His daddy was a lieutenant and said they didn't mind us doing it. We'd have a good time there."

Walter didn't play on any sports teams, but he was often a spectator at athletic events. "Although there were never major league sports here, Charleston always had a minor league baseball team. And all the city parks had recreational adult softball – starting at 7:00, 8:00, 9:00 – an hour-long game. Whoever was ahead at the end of the hour won the game. The teams were sponsored by beer companies and others. There were over forty-five teams. Condon's Department Store and the telephone company sponsored women's teams.

"Boxing was another big thing in town. There was a lot of fleet (Navy ships) coming in, and a lot of the marines and sailors were boxers. So we always had an abundance of boxers. The city sponsored it on the Green (Marion Square). Right across the street, in the bottom of the Knights of Columbus Hall, they had showers so boxers would get ready there and then go over to the Green. If you stood up to watch the fights, you didn't have to pay, and a lot of boys would climb up on John C. Calhoun's monument to see. There was also professional boxing at Sullivan's Sport Bowl. They had a boxing arena up on Race Street. And Charlie Brown, a former boxer, opened up an arena close to where the First Baptist school gym is now in the City Market area. Boxing was the big sport here for many years."

Another source of excitement was, "when I was still a kid, the scouting fleet (destroyers, destroyer tenders and light cruisers) pulled in right along by the Port Authority. We'd go down to the wharves – Graham Wharf, Johnson Wharf – and the Navy would have launchers - small boats - that would take visitors out to the ships. So we'd ride out there to visit the cruisers and destroyers. It was fun."

As for other entertainment, Walter says, "We didn't have much radio, and there was only one radio station – WCSC. It was a local station and it wasn't on a network, so the announcers would get their information out of the local newspaper. They'd sit there and actually read the newspaper on the air! I remember the boys would bring them the paper for the eleven o'clock news. Most people had a Victrola in their homes, so you'd also play records. And you'd invite others in for supper or just walk across the street and sit on the neighbors' doorstep and talk.

"Some friends of my mother used to have a house on the back beach of Sullivan's Island, and we went over there and visited them several times for dinner. Then, when I was a teenager, Mama and my two oldest sisters went in together to buy a house on Sullivan's Island. That was in 1938. I didn't particularly like the beach because it meant I was getting away from the friends I had in the city. I'd be isolated over there, and I was always glad when we came back to town. My younger sister didn't like it either. But the older ones did. We had different interests.

"To get there was a nuisance. The ferry was still running when I was younger. You'd have to get to Sullivan's Island by catching a ferry from the foot of Market Street over to the island. Or you could take one from the city to Mt. Pleasant, then go by bus through the old village in Mt. Pleasant to the island. At that time, the bridge to the island was at Old Cove Inlet and came in at Ft. Moultrie. Once you were on the island, you caught a street car. It went all the way from the fort to the Isle of Palms. That's why you have 'stations' on Sullivan's Island – it's where the street car stops were. But from the time I was nine years old, the Cooper River Bridge was there, so we took the bus most of the time after that. It cost a quarter to get to Sullivan's Island from the city."

Walter remembers that in the city, the biggest entertainment was going to the movies. "It was fairly cheap. You'd go to a movie and see a 'short' (serial) and a news reel and come home to your house and go to bed. In the winter, we'd spend two to three hours at movie theaters to save on heating costs at home. If people were going to a movie, they let their fires burn down in their stoves or fireplaces. A lot of people went three times a week to the movies to save on heating costs."

Walter says his family's house on Wall Street was heated with wood stoves, oil stoves and coal stoves. "We had all three. Most people in Charleston heated with coal. The little doors you see under a lot of the houses were used as coal cellars. You put a couple of pieces in the coal stove, and it would last a long time and give off good heat. Most people in Charleston burned soft coal – bartiminous. It gave out more smoke than hard coal – anthracite - but it was a lot cheaper. Everybody was breathing in the smoke - but do you want to be cold? It was just part of the times."

Walter worked for a while in the office of Johnson's Coal Company at the foot of Laurens Street. "I took calls and was a 'sworn weigher.' Before they loaded the coal, we'd weigh the truck to see what the truck weighed. Then they put the coal on it and we'd weigh it again to see if they were loading the right amount of coal."

When Walter graduated from Bishop England High School in 1939, the city was in the midst of a polio epidemic. "Most of the things in Charleston were cancelled. A lot of the schools - including ours - cancelled their ceremonies. My classmates met at St. Patrick's Church and we had a Mass in the bottom church. Bishop Walsh and Father O'Brien were there and they had asked that the parents not come. I put on my white suit and walked the six or seven blocks from our house to St. Patrick's. My classmate, John McLaughlin, who later became a doctor, had a car and he drove me home afterward." Walter remembers they drove around The Battery before going home, a tradition for anyone who had a car.

Walter says it was a particularly big class that year – about eighty graduates. "People were moving into the state at the time because of the Navy Yard building up, so we had some boys and girls from away. Also, several kids had left school earlier and gotten jobs, then came back to graduate. People would leave if they could get a job because they had to support themselves and their family. Then they'd come back and finish school if they got on their feet. In some cases, they'd just give kids a diploma if they were pretty-well finished because if you could get a job, you'd grab the job. That was all there was to it."

Walter explains that "South Carolina was one of the first places to feel the Depression and one of the last to get over it, although things picked up some when the Santee-Cooper hydroelectric project was constructed. Governor Maybank landed the Santee-Cooper with the help of Senator Jimmy Byrnes, and it was the third biggest project of the New Deal." Another New Deal project was the renovation of the Dock Street Theater. Walter adds, "My mother had the privilege of attending the first play when it opened in 1937. She received an invitation to go because she was president of St. Joseph's PTO. *Time Magazine* and *Life* covered the event and had correspondents there for the grand opening."

Walter says that things really started to look up around Charleston when the Navy Yard expanded. As early as 1910, there was a naval base with a marine barracks in North Charleston. But when President Franklin Roosevelt visited Charleston, U.S. Congressman Thomas McMillan gave him a tour of the relatively small facility and told him that the local authorities wanted shipbuilding facilities here. Walter says, "The president told him to get it through Congress and he'd sign it." The rest is history.

"Long before that, my daddy had worked for awhile at the Dry Dock (where Dockside Condominiums are now)," Walter explains. "During the Second World War, it became the Charleston Shipbuilding and Dry Dock Company. It was a big institution here. It was privately owned and contracted with the Navy. Then the navy yard started expanding, and, to a lesser extent, Ft. Moultrie. So we had a lot of military here. The scouting fleet was still coming in, and the economy had picked up some but it wasn't much. Mayor Lockwood was elected by city council to replace Maybank (who had become governor), and Lockwood started doing some things, too. But he had some arguments back and forth with the admiral at the navy yard because the admiral put the fleet on curfew and they couldn't come downtown. The admiral blamed the city for getting the sailors drunk. Lockwood was one not to be fooled with! He had been a big stevedore."

Walter remembers his sisters talking about the USO dances during WWII. "There were a lot of dances, and my sisters used to go to them. My mother was often a chaperone. The people on the home front had fun. But I was gone a good part of the time because I was in the Marines." Walter says that during the war, there was a POW camp in Moreland, just across the Ashley River Bridge, where about eight-hundred German and Italian prisoners were kept. "Some of the Italians in Charleston used to bring food over to them. I believe there had been a camp there during World War I also."

During the Depression, Walter explains, "We knew there wasn't much money, but it didn't bother us much as kids. Some people in the city even sold wrought iron gates and mantel pieces from many of the old mansions to Northerners. The blacks would talk about the 'po' (poor) 'bukruh' (a Gullah word for white Charlestonians) hanging their wash from clotheslines on piazzas South of Broad. The houses below Broad were nothing beautiful at the time.

"Some people had it worse than others, but most people that we knew had enough to eat. We were never hungry by any means. We didn't have much meat – but we had dishes cooked with meat. And you might have three or four vegetables - okra, tomatoes, corn – for dinner. We always had rice and sometimes ate potatoes in the same meal. On Sunday, we'd have a roast or a chicken. The wagons would pass through the streets and we'd buy two live chickens. Mama would chop the heads off them. And we always had dessert - like banana pudding. I remember every Saturday, my mother made gingerbread - it smelled so good."

Even as children, Walter and his family drank a lot of coffee. "And ice tea," he adds. "We didn't call it 'sweet tea.' Mainly people from the country called it that. But a lot of ladies would sit down and have hot tea in the afternoon."

Walter remembers hearing about people being out of work, but says, "We really didn't suffer much by that. My daddy worked as a machinist. The last job I remember him having was at the bagging mill on Meeting and John Streets. That building later became the Chicco Apartments, and now it is the Hampton Inn. Daddy would sometime walk home for lunch, or we'd bring lunch to him up there. Most men had lunch pails and would have their lunch brought to them. My older brother usually brought the lunch and sometimes I'd go with him."

Walter was pretty small during Prohibition (1918-1933), so he says he mainly remembers just talk of it. "But I do remember once coming out of a corner grocery with my daddy. We passed the sheriff on the street and he went into the store. I don't know why he was going in there. I was a little scared because I'd seen his badge and gun, but Daddy assured me that everything was fine.

"I remember people talking about bootleggers. Sometimes the bootleggers next door to us would move stuff into our yard so the authorities wouldn't find it in their house. And men would come through with wagons yelling 'Any bones, any bottles, any rags!' They'd buy the bottles and sell them to bootleggers to use over again. I picked up a few whiskey bottles and sold them."

Moncks Corner was the center for making bootleg, but there were other rural places that also made it to sell in Charleston. Walter says, "Supposedly, some whiskey made on Edisto Island was so good that it was exported to England. Bootleg whiskey was sold mainly to individuals, but there were some establishments that bought it. And most men made their own beer - home brew. My daddy made it. As kids, we helped - we washed the bottles. We had a machine that would cap the bottles and we had a bench in the kitchen where we kept the beer. Every now and then, one of the bottles would explode and pop off and you'd hear it. Daddy supposedly became pretty good at making home brew. As a kid,

I didn't drink beer, although some of the neighborhood kids did, particularly Germans. They'd have a beer with their lunch. Some places sold a beer called Bevo – a 'near beer' – a half of a percent alcohol. I remember seeing Mama and my oldest brother sitting down having one. And almost everybody made wine. Mama would make scuppernong wine out of raisins.

"As a kid (during Prohibition), I remember the smell of whiskey on people. Most of it was pretty bad stuff. It was hard to get good whiskey in town. You could get it, but it was very costly. Whiskey was all around town. People knew that." Walter says Charleston didn't have speakeasies. "They were mostly in New York. But we had grocery stores where you could drink, and at most organizations – the Elks, Knights of Columbus, Hibernian – there was always somebody who could get whiskey and put it on the table. There were also 'blind tigers.' Ben Tillman had been the governor and they called him the Blind Tiger because he had one bad eye and was a big Clemson man – he didn't like the dudes at The Citadel. Tillman tried to get rid of legal whiskey even before Prohibition. Mama told me that there were some nice places that sold whiskey, and that Tillman would try to close them up. The authorities would come in and smash up the furniture. But the proprietor would just order new furniture and start again. The local constabulary – police - didn't generally enforce laws like that – they didn't care if people drank whiskey or beer."

Walter remembers a story told to him by an older family friend. "Our friend was a doctor and he said that, when he was studying at the medical college in Charleston, the home-made whiskey tasted so bad that, one night, one of the students drank poison by mistake - he thought it was whiskey! He said it tasted about as good as the whiskey! His friends came back and found him and he had to get his stomach pumped. My older brother said they'd take a shot of whiskey and then squeeze a lemon afterward. The main thing was just trying to keep it down. Those were the days when the dudes would carry a fancy flask with them. Even some of the ladies had flasks in their pocketbooks.

"Our friend also said there was a wholesale drug store downtown that had two black men who made gin in the basement. These two fellas supposedly made it better than anybody else. They got good at it because the drug store could always get the supplies. The doctors and pharmacists would go there to pick up medicine, and they'd have a couple of shots of this home-made gin in the basement.

"About 1933 or '34, things changed and stores could legitimately sell beer again. But it was a long time before they could sell whiskey. Finally, you could buy whiskey in a whiskey store but they couldn't pour it in a bar or restaurant. So you'd have to bring your own bottle with you – they called it 'brown-bagging.' It was a long time later that they brought in the mini-bottle."

Walter remembers hearing the story of a shooting in town between two bootleggers. "It happened before I was born. Dunlap was kind of a wholesale bootlegger and Hogan was a retail bootlegger. Dunlap and Hogan were having some words with each other down on Market Street. Dunlap was up in a second-story window with a shotgun, and Hogan was down on the street. Dunlap shot Hogan. It seemed like Hogan may have had a pistol himself, but Hogan was a big fella and Dunlap was a little fella, and Hogan would've beaten the heck out of Dunlap. So they found Dunlap guilty of manslaughter. Russell McGowan came into fame defending Dunlap, and J.C. Long came into fame defending one of the accomplices of Dunlap. J.C. Long was a good lawyer. He got into real estate and got elected to the state senate. Russell McGowan later became the solicitor. Anyway, men would come around to our house and talk to Daddy on the doorstep about the case because he'd been on the jury. McGowan knew Daddy was interested in politics – and he became friendly and sort of a counselor for the family."

Walter's family was always interested in politics. "Daddy worked at the polls during elections and registered people and things like that. My daddy was a close friend of John P. Grace who became mayor of Charleston. They'd grown up together and went to the German Christian Brothers School on Wentworth or Society Street. Then they went to Charleston High School together. John Grace was a figure bigger than life to us. He became the first Irish-American mayor of Charleston. Ironically, more Germans than Irish supported Grace in his second run for office. It probably had something to do with the fact that Grace put Dr. Banov in charge of the health department and Banov ran the cows out of town. Irish women used to keep cows in the city and they sold unpasteurized milk for less than the milk in the stores. So they were upset about losing business.

"Later, during the Maybank and Pinckney mayoral race, Daddy worked for Pinckney, but Maybank won. He was a cotton merchant. When he later became governor, Lockwood, who had been a city councilman, then became mayor. Mayor Morrison came in 1948 or '49. He is the one that gave land to the federal government for the Air Force Base to be built. He also integrated the police force."

Although Walter described neighborhoods as being integrated when he was young, he acknowledges that nothing else was. "Roper Hospital had segregated wards for black patients. St. Francis, the Catholic hospital, would not allow black patients – not even black Catholics! They refused to take Medicare when it was first passed in the mid-1960s because then they'd have to admit black patients." Walter says that there was only one hotel in Charleston for black musicians in the 1940s and '50s – the St. James Hotel on Spring Street where the McDonald's fast-food restaurant is now. "Count Basie and Duke Ellington stayed at the St. James. But a lot of the vaudeville shows couldn't come here because of the lack of places for the black entertainers to stay. Some who did come would stay in homes of black families."

Walter also remembers that "black men were never referred to as 'Mr. So-and-So.' Instead, they were called 'uncle' or 'reverend' or 'doctor.' Or they were called by their first name. Black women were always referred to by their first name. If you referred to a black married couple, it was by their first name and last name – not Mr. and Mrs. But the racial relations were not generally mean-spirited."

Other changes Walter has seen over the years have not been as welcome as the breakdown of racial barriers. "There used to be a grocery store on just about every corner, so you had plenty of stores in easy walking distance. A lot were run by Jewish or German people and a few by Italians. On the corner of Calhoun and Wall Street was a store run by Greeks. On Anson, there was one by Mr. Albenesius. And right across from there was one run by Pulassis. Down Calhoun was a German store. And another German on Alexander was Heissen. Mr. Kessler ran a butcher shop around on Anson and Laurens – a very nice man. So within a few hundred yards, you usually had a store; there was no problem buying groceries. Once we got telephones, you could call them on the phone and they'd send it around to the house."

Another loss, Walter says, is the Clyde Line. "It was a passenger line and used to run from Jacksonville to Charleston to Norfolk to Philadelphia to New York. It would stop a day in each city. People would travel on business or pleasure back in the day when there weren't many airplanes. They would party the whole time! When I had just gotten out of high school, I worked at the Automatic Grocery on the corner of King and Broad Streets. Produce would be sent on the Clyde Line steamship, and we knew there would be a shipment coming into the store when the ship arrived."

Walter also misses a few buildings that have been removed over the years. "There were some nice houses on the corner of George and Meeting Street, across from the College of Charleston gym. There was a beautiful house there made out of brownstone – kind

14

of a Victorian. It had beautiful weeping willow trees in the yard. Metropolitan Life Insurance built a small brick building there in the 1960s. Also, there were two beautiful houses on George Street next to it and they tore those down. Another one that is gone is the Catholic convent on the corner of Legare and Queen. One of my sisters was real smart and had gone to the Academy which was a prestigious school at the convent."

Most of the removal of old buildings has perhaps been in the name of progress. But Walter has seen a few natural disasters impose their will. "Perhaps the biggest storm was in 1938 when I was in high school – the tornado that hit Charleston." The area around the City Market sustained heavy damage. He remembers another big storm – a hurricane - in 1940. "We were on Sullivan's Island at the time and came back into the city when the weather starting getting bad. Generally, we didn't pay much attention to hurricanes and didn't take them as seriously in those days. You didn't have people shouting about them on the radio. There was very little warning, so people didn't worry. Charlestonians were more afraid of cold weather in the winter! They even had a cold wave whistle. At 2:00 in the afternoon, they'd ring the bell in the tower behind the fire station on Meeting and Queen if there was going to be a freeze that night."

Walter's family tree has roots in Charleston dating from the early 1850s. His own life spans over nine decades of Charleston's history. Upon reflection, he says, "Even in poorer times, Charlestonians believed they had a good quality of life. We are much more comfortable now, but are we happier? Who is to say. But we don't want to go any other place. We are where we want to be."

And he often tells people, "Charleston never looked so good."

A WINDOW ON THE WORLD

Clementa Iamundo Florio

Clementa Iamundo Florio was born in Charleston in 1913 and was the oldest of four girls. Her father was an Italian immigrant. "He met my mother here in 1910. She lived on Henrietta Street, right off Meeting by the Citadel Square Baptist Church. My daddy was a band leader in the U.S. Navy for twenty years. He led the band on different ships and would have to leave often on deployments when I was very young. But my mother's family was nearby and would help her when he was gone."

Clementa grew up right across Marion Square from her grandparents, in the thick of things. "We lived upstairs from a store on King Street, four doors from St. Matthew's Lutheran Church. We had big windows and could see everything on the street. They'd have a military parade every year on Armistice Day, and the circus always had a parade down King Street when they'd come to town. The Azalea Festival had a parade and the fair was held across the street on The Green (Marion Square)." One particular cause for celebration that sticks out in Clementa's memory was when Charleston's Mayor Burnet R. Maybank was elected governor in 1938. He was the first Charlestonian to be elected governor since the Civil War. "There was a big parade. Everybody ran down to the corner of Calhoun and King without locking doors or anything. The city went wild! It was grand!"

On a more regular basis, however, movie theaters provided most of the excitement on King Street. And there were quite a few theaters. "There was a movie theater called the Carolina. A nice

Greek man ran it. No movies would show on Sunday in those days, but he'd open the theater at 6 o'clock at night and we'd gather in there. A lot of soldiers would go. He would give them time to sing on the stage for about thirty minutes, and we'd holler and clap for them. They would play music. We had fun. After awhile, he started having a movie at midnight on Sundays. We wanted to go so bad, but Daddy said no.

"Farther up King Street was the Palace Theater. It used to be the Elco but they made it better and named it the Palace. There was also the Lyric Theater. Another was the Princess, but that was closed when I was a child."

Clementa says, "Mostly, you had to create your own entertainment. We never did much, but we were happy, when I think back. We'd go to dime stores on King Street – W.T. Grant, Woolworth. Some of the stores used to have a thing right outside the door that roasted peanuts. You could smell them as you'd walk down King Street – the best smell in the world! A Greek man down the street from us would roast them every afternoon at his store.

"We'd also walk to The Battery and Hampton Park. As teenagers, we used to go to the Francis Marion Hotel – about six of us – and sit on the mezzanine. We'd laugh and talk and cut fool. One afternoon, the manager came over and said we were too loud. He said, 'I don't mind you young people being here, but if you continue to make so much noise, you'll have to leave.' We must have been bothering people in the restaurant."

From the windows of her family's apartment overlooking King Street, Clementa would see black peddlers coming through pushing carts and selling fish, produce and other foods. They'd sing as they came through to rouse up potential customers. During the Azalea Festival, she says all of the black peddlers went to The Battery for a contest to determine which vendor had the best song. She also remembers, "We used to see the real 'Porgy' (Sammy Smalls) in his cart pulled by a goat. He used to ride through King Street."

Clementa says that, every day, the black news boy would come along chanting "News and Core-ee-ohhh." And they'd run through screaming "Extra, Extra" if there was any big news. "Like the 7th of December, 1941, we were coming back from a day trip up the country. You always had to drive down King Street when you were in a car before you went home. It was barely getting dark – about 6:00 - and we heard all the yelling – 'Extra Extra.' That's how we found out about the attack on Pearl Harbor."

Clementa was a child in the 1920s, so she remembers a little about Prohibition. "A lot of people made wine for their own use. Before Daddy started making wine, some of his friends used to make it. One of his friends – an Italian - had a little grocery store – and Daddy used to send my sister and me around there with a little note asking him if he had wine. The man would put it in a shopping bag with two handles and we'd carry it home together. One evening, one of the neighbors saw us two kids struggling with the shopping bag and offered to help us get it home. My daddy told us not to ever let anybody see what was in the bag. So we kept insisting that we could get it home by ourselves.

"My best friend's daddy had a store on King Street. My sister and I would go there to buy home-made wine for my daddy, too. He would also put apples and oranges in the bag. Sometimes my sister went by herself. One day, she didn't come home right away, so I went to her friend's house looking for her. There was the shopping bag sitting inside the fence and nobody around! So I went in and told my sister, 'You've got to come home' but she said, 'No, I am playing ball.' I said, 'What about this package of groceries? You've got to come home!' I finally got her to leave.

"Italians were big on parties so Daddy made wine in big jugs. You had to leave the jugs open because you'd have to let the wine boil or ferment. We were living above the store on King Street - a real nice Jewish man ran it. One time, one of those jugs boiled over and the wine ran down through our floor and into the store - into the boys' clothes department! Purple wine was all over the clothes! We discovered it first while our parents were still sleeping. That was the first time I ever saw my daddy scared. He kept saying, 'Oh they're going to lock me up – I'm going to jail.' It was early and the store was still closed. Daddy told my aunt, 'You go down and talk to Mr. Snyder. Tell him I'll pay for it.' Where he'd ever get the money, I don't know. But Mr. Snyder told my aunt, 'Tell him not to worry about it. Just give me a gallon of wine when it's ready.' Daddy made sure he got the gallon of wine! And he gave the clothes to Auntie – I remember she had them hanging on the line drying. I don't know what they did with them because they were ruined!"

Clementa had a girlfriend who lived south of the City Market. "Her daddy owned a little grocery store down there where fellas could sit in and drink. He was a fisherman, and his wife would run the business when he was gone. Mostly other fisherman came in and would sit around the store and drink. She served liquor right from the grocery counter. My daddy didn't like me to go down there to see my girlfriend because he said Market Street was a bad street. But we went anyway. You know her daddy wouldn't have left his family if it were anything bad. Sometimes it would be almost dark and we'd be walking back home, but nobody bothered us. There was a lot of empty space in the Market. A couple of people had meat markets in that area, and black people had their vegetables for sale, but there just wasn't much else there."

Clementa's father used to go to the dock near there and pick up things he'd ordered from New York. "It would come in on the ships. We liked that because he'd get big baskets of apples and big boxes of spaghetti and cans of olive oil. They'd last for awhile – everything but the apples because we'd eat them up right away!"

When Clementa's father retired from the Navy, he was a member of the Philharmonic Orchestra in Charleston. "The conductor was Mr. Wichman who also taught music. My daddy played in the orchestra for twenty years. They played good music. They'd have one concert a year, but they'd practice all year for that one concert! Every Monday night he'd have to go to practice. He played the French horn. He also could play the piano. But none of us played music. He was going to have an all-girl orchestra with his four daughters, but he'd laugh at us even trying to sing. Finally, he gave up and said, 'Y'all are making me look like a damn fool – I quit.' We said thank goodness!"

Clementa's father taught music to several pupils who did take an interest in it. He used the living room for the lessons. "There was one man who used to come every Sunday, and he taught him to play the clarinet. But most of his students were children of his friends.

"People called my daddy 'the band master.' He wanted to have his own band when he got out of the service but never got it. But he kept up with the music. There was a man who had a dance band – Carl Metz – and he was in that. In the summertime at the parks, they used to play. There were eight concerts in the summer at The Battery and Hampton Park. That was in the 1920s and early 30s."

Clementa lived in the upstairs apartment on King Street for fifteen years. "We were there when I got married, and my husband and I stayed there with my parents for awhile. Then he and I moved to the Meeting Street Manor up by Aiken Street when my first child was a babe in arms. They had just opened up, so they were all new apartments. A good many residents were navy yard workers.

The federal government started it, but then the city took it over. It was built for people with lower income. There was a road that ran through the middle of the complex, and white people lived on one side and black people lived on the other side."

Clementa's view from the windows of her childhood home on upper King Street reflects a time when that area was full of the hustle-and-bustle of everyday Charleston - and sometimes a little added excitement. As is sometimes the case, things have come full circle for upper King Street, and it is once again thriving and a hub of activity.

Even though the view has changed a bit.

SHARED MEMORIES

George and Bertha (Lazarus) Breibart

At 95 years old, George Breibart's memories spanning nearly a century in Charleston are very vivid.

"I was born in 1917 at 729 Meeting Street. When I was two years old, my father built a corner grocery store a couple of doors away at 739 Meeting, between Maple and Indian Street (or First Street, they called it). From then on, we lived over the store. My sister was born when we lived above the store. In those days, the doctor came to the house. We had a phone in the store but a lot of people didn't have phones. So if you wanted a doctor and had no car or phone, you'd come to Mr. Sam's store – my daddy. They'd come and say, 'The baby is coming – will you call the doctor?'

"Our grocery store was like a meeting place, and men from the neighborhood would hang around - both black and white men. Our neighborhood had a mixture of black and white families in it. There were no problems. But one time, we saw a cross burning behind the house across the street. The man who lived there was a Catholic, and there was prejudice against them. So we didn't know if the cross-burning was meant for him or for the blacks or for us, the Jews! That was in the 1920s."

George's father was from Russia and came to Charleston via New York. "At first, my parents lived with my uncle on Alexander Street. My brother, Sol, was born in 1914 when my parents lived there with my aunt and uncle. My brother wrote a lot about the Jewish history in Charleston and has been quoted in a number of things. He did a tremendous amount of research and loved history. His wife donated all his books to the College of Charleston library." (Note: The S.C. Jewish Historical Society keeps its records there.) "My brother is buried in the Jewish cemetery on Coming Street, across from the building that used to be a Catholic school for black kids."

George attended James Simons Grammar School. "I remember looking out the classroom window and watching them build the extension of the Enston Homes (for the elderly). Our classrooms were right across the street from it. I walked to school most of the time, but my parents took me in the car when I went to high school." George graduated from Charleston High School in 1933 at a time when only boys attended it.

"When I was in high school, I worked at the store," George says. "I didn't play sports. There was not much time for play. But I played music and was in the high school orchestra. We practiced two or three times a week at the Circular Church or Hibernian Hall. We went to competitions in Rock Hill and won a couple of times. I took violin lessons from Mr. Wichman who taught at Charleston High School. He had a studio at 123 Meeting Street near the Gibbes Art Gallery. In the summertime, I'd ride there on the streetcar for three cents. He had a woman assistant and would have individual lessons but also had us get together like an orchestra. Mr. Wichman was a real dedicated musician, and he conducted the Charleston Symphony which was called the Philharmonic in those days. As a teenager, sometimes he'd let you sit in the back of the symphony and play with them. He was always trying to raise money to keep it going. He was a very generous man when it came to music. During the war, they investigated him and his brother just because they were German. Mr. Wichman lived on Sullivan's Island and came in on the ferry every morning because there was no bridge. I remember when they built the

Grace Bridge in 1929. He got the boys from the orchestra and we all walked over it before it opened."

George says, "My oldest brother also took music lessons but he took from Mr. Metz who taught brass instruments. Mr. Metz was the band leader at The Citadel. He had a studio, too. My brother learned to play the saxophone. My brother went further than I did and played in local bands. And when he went to UNC, he played in their band."

Two or three days a week after school, George went to Hebrew school. "I rode the bus to the little shul (synagogue), Beth Israel. It was a small wooden building at 145 St. Philip Street, in the block between Morris and Radcliffe Streets. It sat back off the street. In more recent years, it was some kind of Masonic building. Beth Israel was an Orthodox synagogue, and most of the members were immigrants – first generation here – and hadn't Americanized as much as the others. It was established sometime between 1900 and 1920. The men were all hard workers. My father was a hard worker. He kept long hours at the store. It wasn't a big business – just a mom-and-pop grocery.

"At that time there wasn't too much up in the north part of the city where I grew up. It was an industrial area. There was a fertilizer plant on King and Simons Streets, and for many years, there was an abattoir (slaughterhouse) on Meeting near Mt. Pleasant Street - where the Longshoremen's building is now." George says he has some recollection of cattle being herded on Meeting Street, undoubtedly being led to slaughter. "The stench when the animal refuse was being burned was unbelievable!"

Another early memory for George was being on Calhoun Street one day in 1927 and hearing the newsboy yelling, "Extra! Extra!" as he came through the street with a special edition. Charles Lindbergh had just completed his historic trans-Atlantic flight! "This was even before radio," he says. Because there was no radio in those days, real-time plays of the World Series were shown via a visual display board set up for the public to see at the Charleston Evening Post's building across from the Gibbes Art Gallery. George explains, "They had a board built like a baseball field in front of the building. Plays were shown as soon as they happened by moving pieces around on the board. It was very easy to follow the action."

George's friends were mostly neighborhood kids. "Our shul didn't have youth groups in those days and there were not many Jews living in our area. The Jewish neighborhoods were down around King and Warren Streets. Also on St. Philip Street and around Rutledge Avenue. I had friends in school, but some said we couldn't visit back and forth because I was Jewish. I always felt like a minority. My younger brother couldn't get in at the medical college here in Charleston because of restrictions on Jews. They had a quota. But one teacher in high school took a liking to him and said 'If you want to get into medical school, I'll get you into Duke.' So he went to Duke. Even in 1972, when we bought our house, they wouldn't sell to Jews if they knew."

George recalls, "When I was real young, there were a number of Jewish families living on lower King Street. In the summer, people – especially Jewish people - would go to The Battery, right across the street from where the Fort Sumter Hotel is. Summertime was hot, and in the evening when it cooled off, families would all go there and the children would run around. My wife Bertha's family had moved from Charleston to Summerville when she was five or six, but one summer she was staying with family friends on lower King Street, and I saw her at The Battery." Later, when Bertha was grown and working at the Charleston Linen Service (on Meeting Street, between John and Ann Streets), she rode in to work every day from Summerville with a woman who brought four or five people to town every day. "My mother used to bring Bertha to lunch at our house. My mother was working on it (matchmaking)!"

Bertha's family attended Brith Sholom Orthodox Synagogue when it was on St. Philip Street – where the College of Charleston's Fine Arts building is today. The Jewish Community Center was there also. George explains, "The AZA was a very active group for young Jewish people (ages 17-21). They put on dances there. Even some of the real religious ones loved to sing and dance. They believed in making religion a happy event."

George acknowledges there wasn't much extra money when he was young, particularly in the northern section of the city where he lived. "But my parents had a maid, even though it was the Depression. They paid her $2.50 a week to come get the kids ready for school and to cook and clean. At that time, the WPA (FDR's Works Progress Administration) came in and made some jobs, and people were making $1.25 a week – just enough to get by. Some were very small jobs. For instance, on road construction crews, one guy would take a shovel of dirt and walk it down to the other corner, just to give him a job. The CCC (FDR's Civilian Conservation Corps) tried to get the young people a little something – cleaning the beach or something. The government didn't give food stamps, but sometimes they'd pay people in 'script' and you could buy stuff with it. People could get so much in groceries a week in script. My father had some of that business. The welfare board apportioned so much money to his store once or twice a month. We'd deliver groceries to people who had it – five pounds of grits, one pound of sugar, a box of smoked heron, five pounds of flour, butt meat – that was the cheapest thing you could buy. But you couldn't use script for any frivolous things."

When the war came along, George and Bertha were already married. "We got married in 1941. We had to wait to get married because houses were so short (scarce). I had a friend who was going to move, so we finally found a place. The Oakman Drug Store people owned a few buildings where the Rutledge Tower of the Medical University is now. The old St. Francis hospital was also there. There was a grocery store on the corner, and there were some beautiful three-story houses and a two-story one. We had an apartment on the bottom of one."

Shortly after the war, a new Conservative synagogue was founded in the city. "The Steinbergs bought an old surplus army building – a wooden building - and set it up on Gordon Street. It was on a beautiful lot. This synagogue (Emanu-El) was a little bit more liberal than Brith Sholom. Women and men could sit together. Then Beth Israel put up a big new building on Rutledge Avenue. They needed to increase membership so they merged with Brith Sholom. Brith Sholom had been established about 1850. They were a break-off from KKBE (Kahal Kadosh Beth Elohim) on Hasell Street which is Reform. Reform is more Americanized. KKBE was the first Reform synagogue in America." George adds a little more Jewish history: "On Broad Street, next to the courthouse, you can look up on one of the buildings and see the Star of David. The Hebrew Orphan Society was there at one time. They still have the society - I got a notice the other day they were holding a meeting."

Although Bertha and George both belonged to Orthodox families, it was difficult to keep a kosher household. Bertha says that when her family lived in Summerville, she had a brother who came to Charleston every day to pharmacy school at the medical college. "We were trying to keep kosher at home, so he'd bring a live chicken on the train on his way to school and he'd leave it at a certain grocery store. They would slaughter it and then he'd pick it up before going back home on the train to Summerville. He didn't like it, but he did it!"

When Bertha was small, her family lived for several years below Broad Street at 77 King Street where her father's shoe repair business was located. They later moved to upper King Street near Cannon Street and then to Summerville. "There were other shops like his in Charleston so there wasn't enough business for him here," she explains. Summerville had about 3,000 people when

Bertha's family lived there in the 1930s. She attended public schools there. After high school, she went to Rice Business College in Charleston, on the corner of Broad and King. It was a secretarial school. Then she got a job as a clerk in the office at the Charleston Linen Service on Meeting Street. Bertha remembers that there was a candy store nearby on John Street and that its employees would throw candy out the window to passersby. She also remembers that the employees of the Linen Service went on a weekend trip to Myrtle Beach each year, and her picture was in the paper once with her co-workers on the outing.

But that wasn't the only time her picture was in the paper. In 1935, Bertha was chosen to be Miss Summerville. She says she didn't want to enter the contest, but several people persuaded her mother to push her. "She was the prettiest and won," George boasts. But Bertha insists, "The thing that won the contest was the gown I wore. My mother and I went to Belk and everywhere else looking for one. Then we found a gorgeous white chiffon. I knew that would probably win it. I think it was the dress. But I didn't think I was going to get that dress because it was still the Depression. I felt bad having my mother spend all that money for it."

After being crowned Miss Summerville, it was onto the Miss Azalea contest which was held in Charleston during the city's Azalea Festival. Bertha explains that the annual affair was "a pretty big thing - street dances and big bands in the middle of King Street. Some of the halls like the Hibernian also had bands. When we came to Charleston, we stayed in the Francis Marion Hotel. I didn't want to go. I didn't especially like it. We were there almost a week, I think. It was too much. I wasn't used to being away from home. If I'd been a little older, I would've appreciated it a little more, but I was seventeen. And we had the same thing every morning for breakfast – potatoes!"

George remembers that, when Bertha was living in Summerville, a hurricane hit Charleston. "In those days, you didn't know when there was going to be a hurricane. Bertha didn't know about it because they didn't have a radio. So she came into Charleston for work that day! At the time, I was in Florida with a friend and we were driving back to Charleston. When I got home to the store, my family was on the second floor bailing out water. The storm peeled the whole tin roof off our store and left it in the street."

George remembers a little about Prohibition, too. "A lot of politics was mixed in. I remember many of the cops themselves would bring in the moonshine. One of the lead dogs (policemen) had moonshine in the back of his car. It was quite prevalent. A lot of the stores in Charleston had whiskey, and if they had moonshine, they had customers! There was a lottery, too. Stores had ball machines – they never confiscated the ball machines. We had a slot machine in the back of our store - even in the poorest of times."

Another sign of the times was that "people had horses and wagons in their back yard. There was even a water trough for the horses on John Street. That's where they had drays – wagons." Men with wagons could be hired for hauling things.

Street peddlers, known locally as "hucksters," were another common site. George explains, "There was a knife sharpener who would ride through on his bicycle. He had a little emery wheel on the back of it to sharpen knives. He'd holler, 'Knife sharpener, knife sharpener' every time he'd come around. I also remember organ grinders standing on street corners. They had a little monkey wearing a little hat. They weren't local people. They travelled from place to place."

A real treat for George was when "my father used to take the family to get ice cream at a drug store in the Timrod Hotel on Meeting Street, across from Washington Park. The Ashley Ice

Cream Company would come around to the grocery stores and deliver it, too. In our store, we had a wooden chest with a metal container inside it for the ice cream. They'd come every day to repack it with ice."

George explains, "A lot of things people would buy in our store wasn't packaged then. We had to scoop it up – flour, rice, sugar. There were some places that just sold meat – one on King near Liberty; one on Rutledge and Spring - the Avenue Market. The man who started the Piggly Wiggly here had a meat market on President and Cannon Streets during the war.

"The German immigrants were the first to have corner stores," George says. "Then the Greeks and the Jews came over. Most didn't have a trade or anything so they opened a business." George went into business with his father when he finished high school. "My mother was sick, and my father needed help. I ran the grocery store for 47 years."

George was away from Charleston for several years when he served in the Army during World War II. "After the war, we couldn't get a place downtown to rent so we lived for a while with her father in Summerville. I'd ride back and forth to my father's store in Charleston with a guy who was a mechanic, and on the weekends, I'd take the bus. Then we bought a house in Byrnes Down. They were new houses – built in 1947.

George and Bertha

31

We were the second family to own that house – we paid $8500 for it! There were at least a dozen Jewish families living in Byrnes Down. But once we moved out of the city, I was never so Orthodox that I'd walk back downtown to synagogue!"

These days, the building on upper St. Philip Street where George's small shul had been is converted to condominiums. His father's store is now a beauty parlor. Bertha's synagogue has been torn down and the property is enveloped by the College of Charleston. The site of the Charleston Linen Service, where she worked for several years as a young girl, is the parking lot for the Charleston Visitor Center. Together, George and Bertha have seen the past nine decades bring huge changes to this city. Some people would say it's not even the same city. But a city is more than just bricks and mortar.

It is people like the Breibarts.

EVERY PICTURE TELLS A STORY
William F. (Buddy) Bendt

If a picture is worth a thousand words, ask Buddy Bendt to show you his sketch of "My Neighborhood's Sunset, 1936." It tells the story of the street where he spent the first fifteen years of his life – uptown on Meeting Street between Romney and Poinsett Streets. "I tried to sketch it out to keep from forgetting," he says. It's hard to believe Buddy Bendt would forget anything!

Buddy was born in 1921, the third of four children. "We lived with my mother's parents at 755 Meeting Street. At the time, there was a church on the corner. These days, the entire block belongs to the church, and they built a new church right where we lived. My drawing shows how things used to look the day we moved away from that old house."

Buddy explains, "It was a mixed neighborhood. A lot of neighborhoods had black and white families. The black children that lived down the alley had their own school and we went to James Simons School. We didn't play together, and they mostly stayed to themselves. But we had no troubles. I had a first cousin – three years younger – whose family would come to visit us. We wouldn't see him in the yard, so we'd ask the black lady next door if she'd seen him. He'd be there playing with her children or in their kitchen eating dinner. Nobody squawked about it."

In 1930, there were eleven people living in Buddy's two-story house. "Everybody in my family lived there – my grandmother and grandfather, a couple of uncles were there. My grandfather retired from the power company (SCE&G) and got $20 a month. He had gotten hurt and at first they put him on light duty; then he retired. They also gave him a small plot down at SCE&G where he could do a little gardening."

Buddy walked to school "across the railroad tracks and past Factory Hill. That's where the people who worked in the bagging mill lived. It was next to County Hall on King Street. The bagging mill was where County Hall is now. Everybody in my neighborhood walked to school that way. It was about three quarters of a mile. Later, I rode a bicycle to Murray Vocational High School over by Colonial Lake. I never rode to school in a car or a bus in my life."

Buddy says, "I didn't stay long at Murray. I wanted to go to work. You can betcha we had very little. My folks would've seen to it that I got my education, but I was seventeen and had a hard head, so instead I went to the shipyard to see about getting a job. They told me I had to be eighteen, so the next day, I went back and lied – I told them I was eighteen. At first, I went to work as a classified laborer which meant I worked with gangs of people shoveling dirt. I made $17 a week. I never had so much money in all my life! About six months later, they called me to the office and gave me a job where I had to go around and check on where people were working and to keep track of money. They liked me, and I liked them."

During the Depression, Buddy says "people hardly had enough money to eat. I had a friend whose daddy worked for the city. On pay day, they gave him script. Then, when the city had money, they could cash in the script and get money. All the grocery stores recognized script as money, and they'd take it. On Saturday nights, we'd be treated to a little glass of milk. We looked forward to it. We didn't have it during the week. Two summers, when I was twelve or so, I went with my friend to his aunt and uncle's house in the country. They had a dairy farm, and we had all the milk we could drink!"

Buddy remembers, "There was a lottery during the Depression. I was a little fellow, but my grandma would give me a dime and tell me to go down to a tiny wooden office behind the car barn and put the money on the name of 'Mary.' They had a number for 'Mary.' Many times, my grandmother would win $10 off a dime. They weren't crooks, and they were running it honestly. I'm sure the authorities knew all about it and left it alone."

Buddy says the car barn and the little lottery office were only two blocks away from his house on Meeting Street. "The car barn is where they kept the streetcar or trolley car. The streetcars ran on electricity from a cable overhead - it seemed to float along. The streetcar used to run on King Street and would come up as far as Cleveland Street - by County Hall - and make a turn and go by Hampton Park. Then it would swing around and come back out. Another route rode from The Battery all the way to North Charleston. They also had the belt line which circled around the city. I saw the last streetcar go into the car barn. The car barn is still there today, but it's run down."

As a kid, Buddy went to Hampton Park quite often, "especially on Sunday afternoons. It had a zoo. I remember the monkeys most. But there were no playgrounds up our way. We played baseball at a field up on Brigade Street. We just had neighborhood make-up teams. There were a lot of good ball players and the bigger boys taught us. There were two big oak trees on the corner of Meeting and Williman Street - I call that corner 'Twin Oaks College!' We also played half rubber. You use half of a rubber ball and a broom stick. We'd take turns being pitcher, catcher and batter. We also went swimming in the Cooper River at the 'Y' which is where the trains would back up into Union Station on Columbus Street. And we swam at a place called Red Shed where the railroad track crossed a creek on the way to that Y."

The American Legion sponsored a baseball team on which Buddy played. "We used to play against the orphan house team on the

Citadel Green (Marion Square). The Green was all pebbles then. And it wasn't green. You couldn't slide into a base.

"When I was twelve, I broke my arm playing baseball. I was in old Roper Hospital for six weeks! I stayed in a ward with other patients. Well, with a broken arm, I was all over the hospital exploring. I peeped into the operating room and saw all kinds of things in there. I got downstairs where they were doing an autopsy on a man using a hammer and chisel on the top of his head. I didn't stay there very long! Sometime they'd see me and say 'Get on back to where you belong.' Anyway, the ward started filling up and they put the beds closer together. Then, I got the flu, so they moved my bed to the middle of the floor. One day, the nurses came and started moving my bed. I said, 'Where are you taking me?' They said, 'We're going to take you to the dayroom.' The dayroom was where families could come visit patients who were going to die. Rather than let a patient die in the ward, they'd move them to the dayroom. Man, I came outa that bed! So they understood and rolled me back to the middle of the ward and took someone else to the dayroom."

Buddy remembers that, "around Charleston, big companies had their own baseball teams for their employees. I heard if there was a good baseball player, the company would hire him just so he could play on the team. Many a time, I sat and watched my uncles play for Standard Oil. I don't remember who had the rest of the teams, but the Marines also had a team. When my uncles would be playing the Marines, my grandmother and I would take the streetcar up to the navy base and watch them there. But one time, I remember my friend and I left the Palace Theater and hurried over to see the ball game on Hagood Avenue. They had a baseball field over there where The Citadel's football stadium is now. We didn't have any money to get in, so we went under the fence. After the game, we were afraid to leave through the main gate, so we crawled back out under the fence!"

For most kids in Buddy's time, the biggest entertainment was going to the movies. "The famous theater was the Palace. It was on the east side of King, just south of Spring Street. There is a vacant lot there now. Grandma always had a handkerchief with a little change tied up in the corner, and she would give me ten cents to go. You'd see a cowboy show, cartoons, coming attractions and a few other little things and have a nickel left to buy a candy bar. The shows never ended – you could go in anytime and it was always running. Many a time, I'd go with a friend and we'd say, 'Let's leave now' when it got to the part where we had come in."

Buddy remembers an annual event was the Schutzenfest, a German festival that was held uptown at the Rifle Club. "Our neighbor would make a wooden eagle and it would be set up in the marsh on a barge. You'd get a shotgun and whoever knocked the head off the eagle won. They also had races for the children. And upstairs in the building was a dance hall. I think that's where I saw the band, the Ink Spots. One time they had a walkathon in there. People stayed on their feet as long as they could. You could go there all hours and see them. They'd be struggling to stay on their feet!"

When Buddy's family left the neighborhood in his drawing, they moved briefly to 3 Maple Street. Soon afterward, his grandfather died and they then moved with his grandmother to a house on Williman Street, three blocks north of Romney, on the east side of Meeting. "There was an apartment upstairs and an apartment down-stairs. The Rosens owned it and a few other houses on the street. Mr. Rosen had bought the lumber when they were tearing down the barracks after the First World War, and he built several houses using that wood. We lived in the upstairs apartment for almost ten years. It was a true neighborhood – everybody knew everybody."

Buddy says his family was living there when the tornado hit Charleston in 1938. "There wasn't enough room for me to stay with my family, so I slept down the street with my aunt and uncle and their three boys. They had a tiny bedroom upstairs in the back. I remember that morning a terrible wind and rain started up. Like a nut, I stood at the back window and looked out! I could see tin, all kind of junk, flying by. Next thing you knew, it was over. The sun came out! The tornado took Sacred Heart Church and twisted it, so it had to come down after that. They used to have services in James Simons School's auditorium until the new church was built. It completely destroyed the rectory and the church hall, too. That tornado also took down Woodstock which was a company that made crates for Coca Cola, and it took down William Gable Company. They produced furniture. Before then, when I was a kid, sometimes the sawdust pile there would get to be ten feet high, and we would play on that thing. Then they would spread it all out and, before you knew it, was high again."

Buddy was living on Williman Street when he enlisted in the Army during World War II. "When we came back after the war, the first thing we tried to do was to get a date. We went to the Idle Hour – that was one of our places - on King Street by Romney. It was a nightclub – very nice. They didn't have bands - they had a piccolo (juke box). But first, I had to buy clothes. I had plenty of green underwear, so I sure didn't need to buy any underwear! The government gave everybody $100, and I went to where I always bought my clothes – J. Needle – a men's clothing store on King Street, across from the Palace Theater. The government gave me a hundred dollars for each of the next two months, so each month I'd buy me a suit. I ended up with three new suits! I'd gone back to work at the Navy Yard, too, and I always gave my grandmother half of what I made there.

"After being home for six months, I met my wife, Dorothy. She was working at Kress on King Street. Her sister worked at the Cigar Factory. The Cigar Factory was at the east end of Columbus Street. It employed mostly women and kept many a family with food and clothing. The Cigar Factory was the best source of a job there was.

A lot of women came in from the country to work there. My wife and her sister came from Cottageville. There must've been 600-700 people working at the Cigar Factory, and it must've been there for eighty-five or ninety years. My aunt went to work there when she was fourteen and stayed there forty-five or fifty years. There were all kinds of jobs there. My aunt ran a machine. My wife's sister worked with shades of cigars and had to make sure all the cigars in the box were the same shade. She got to where she could pick that shade out right quick. One would be a little darker, so it'd go in with the darker ones. A little lighter, it'd go in with the lighter ones. One of the cigars was called Cremo – and the factory became known by locals as Cremo College!"

Buddy and Dorothy

Buddy's father was in the grocery business, but not in the usual sense of the word. He says that in those days, there were grocery stores on just about every corner. "Right across the street from us was Baker's and down on the other corner was Stuart. Another block up was Rudick's, another was Rosen and another was Feldman. When the stores would put on sales or specials, they would call on my daddy to draw a sign on the window in the front. He'd get outside with some kind of marker and would write the words on the window in beautiful lettering – and he was very good at it."

One look at Buddy's drawing of his old neighborhood makes it clear that he has inherited that artistic gene. And since every picture tells a story, maybe we can get him to draw a few more pictures.

LITTLE MEXICO

Rutledge and Inez Spalviero Cox

If you ever need a reason to believe in fate and premonitions, meet Rutledge and Inez Cox. They both grew up in Little Mexico, the area of the city today known as the East Side, but they didn't know each other as children. "I was born in 1924 and she was born in 1928. I am an old goat," Rutledge declares. It wasn't until after he returned home from the Merchant Marines that he met Inez, rather by accident. She explains, "I worked with his sister in a doctor's office, and Rutledge was in the car one day when somebody gave both of us girls a ride home. Rutledge had just come home from the Merchant Marines - and there he was! Then he started calling and worrying me to death." The couple has been married for 62 years.

It must have been fate. Rutledge travelled the world, only to come home and meet the proverbial girl next door. But the premonition actually came much earlier. "Rutledge's daddy bought our store from us when I was a baby," Inez says. "Rutledge was four years old at the time, and I was told he looked at me in the crib and said something. But I don't know what he said." Could it have been a promise perhaps? Rutledge claims he doesn't remember.

Rutledge's family has lived in Charleston for several generations. "My father was born in Little Mexico at 34 Blake Street. His grandparents came from the area down by the port. They lived at 41 Concord Street. There were mainly buildings down there catering to shipping interests. My grandfather worked as a printer and at one time as a baker. My grandfather had two sons who were sail makers off Vendue Range. A lot of the docks were down there then and that's where life was.

"The first job I ever heard of my daddy having was in the early 1920s at the Navy Yard. Then he got involved in the grocery business. Corner groceries were a big thing in those days. But he got out of that and went to work at the American Tobacco Company – the Cigar Factory. He was a foreman in the box department – making boxes. Then he left that and opened a little grocery store at 16 Reid Street - on the corner of Reid and Drake. That's the one he took over from Inez's father."

Rugledge was born at 35 ½ Blake Street, "a little house right behind my daddy's first grocery store. Dr. Jaegar came around and delivered me. You'll see his picture hanging at Roper Hospital. There is also one there of Dr. Rutledge. He was a head doctor and all the other doctors knew him. Dr. Jaegar suggested that my family name me for Dr. Rutledge because he thought so much of him.

Rutledge behind their store

So I was named for Dr. Rutledge. I got my middle name, Eugene, after Dr. Eugene Jaeger.

"Anyway, all six of us kids were born in that little cottage. It had three rooms - a bedroom, a parlor and a kitchen, but I never saw a bathroom. It must've been outside. I wasn't old enough to remember. In the oldest picture ever made of me, I am holding a bag of candy behind our first store."

Rutledge's family later moved above the Reid Street store his father bought from Inez's father. "I lived there until my father died of double pneumonia," Rutledge says. "Then my mother got a job at the Cigar Factory. I remember the white workers used to wear white and green uniforms, and the black workers wore blue and brown. I was five years old at the time. I was the youngest boy, so my aunt took me to live with her at 75 America Street. My mother kept the other two boys, and someone else took care of my three sisters. But we were all still in the same area as the rest of my father's family," so Rutledge was able to spend time with his brothers and sisters. "I remember my brother and I used to go out to the jetties in a little rowboat and go fishing. My brother was five years older than me and was pretty sea-worthy. We'd sit on the jetties. They were slick and slimy and you better be careful because you could easily slip into the water!"

Generations of Rutledge's family attended St. John's Episcopal Church in Little Mexico, on the corner of Amherst and Hanover Streets. "We followed the queen," he quips. "My father is buried there and most of his family were married and buried there. My great-grandfather is buried right under the church. They needed more room so they built some space over some of the graves. I could show you right now at the edge of the church the original grave stone in the floor and you can read his name."

Little Mexico had everything Rutledge needed – or wanted – as a kid. "I never liked to wander too much out of the neighborhood. And anybody new that came through, we'd have to check him out. Mall Playground was on America Street, across from where Our Lady of Mercy Catholic Church is. It was a good size park, and you couldn't drive a car through America Street like you can now. Then they tore down all the houses – about ten of them - on the east side of the street and built a high school for black kids. Our neighborhood had a mixture of black and white families living there. Sometimes the black and white kids played together. You know, boys would play with boys to get something going. Their school (C.A. Brown High School) is now the Palmer Campus of

Trident Tech, behind the old Cigar Factory. I can tell you who lived in all the houses that are gone now."

Rutledge recollects a few particular events in his neighborhood that made an impression on him as a young boy. One was when a foot of water came up in his aunt's store during a hurricane in the 1930s. "Everything in the store was floating around. All that land is low – a block or two over from the Cooper River."

And Rutledge says that when he was about fourteen years old, "I remember I was on Columbus Street and happened to look up at a car that came through. It was President Franklin Roosevelt with Mayor Maybank sitting on his right and Governor Johnson on his left. Nobody in the neighborhood knew he was coming through, and just a few people on the street at the time saw it. But here he comes in a convertible! He was probably coming from the train station which was at the foot of Columbus Street. It got my attention!"

Almost every Charlestonian alive at the time remembers the day in 1938 when multiple tornadoes hit the city. "My brother happened to be working down at the Market. He told me that people were buried in the piles of brick and that he was getting jerked all around to help get them out. He'd be doing one thing then they'd call him over to do something else."

Although he was quite young during Prohibition, Rutledge remembers a few signs of the time. "There was an officer called Pompey who went around on a bicycle. He was also a truant officer and had other duties. But when the word got out that Pompey was coming, people would start tearing the wood siding off their houses and putting the whiskey bottles down in there. Then they'd nail the boards back on real good and say 'Pompey can't get this! He'd need a hammer to get this off!' They'd bring in moonshine from Berkeley County on the train. They'd say 'Get as near to Charleston as you can, and throw it off the train into the marshy areas before you pull in. Then go back in the car and pick it up.' They'd bring it to my neighborhood and fill up the bottles in the bathtub and look out for Pompey to come. If he came into a house that had it, he'd squirt something in the bathtub and ruin the whiskey."

Rutledge says, "My daddy's mother was a Dunlap. One of her relatives took charge of selling whiskey all over town. He got shot and was partially blinded from it. I think he shot someone and then got shot by someone else. Must've been a bad deal – short money or something. Another relative, Leon Dunlap, ran the Idle Hour on King Street."

Rutledge remembers, "People also made home brew. They'd throw the bottles under the house to let it get seasoned – to let it brew. They'd line them up in the sand under the house to age. Aging is a big factor. People also made root beer and put it under the house to age. You'd hear the bottle caps popping off a lot in the summertime."

Rutledge lived with his aunt until he was sixteen. She ran a grocery store at 97 America Street which coincidentally was back-to-back with the house he was born in at 35 ½ Blake. "I helped a lot in her store growing up. She was married but had no kids of her own. Her husband was a steam engineer for the railroad. Nobody had any money and if you were running a grocery store, it was hard to keep it going. But my aunt managed to give me a membership at the YMCA at 26 George Street. There was a pool, a track, and a rec room. I went with the YMCA to the world's fair in New York when I was sixteen. We went on a school bus - it was a rough ride, and took two or three days. It cost $50 to go, but I told my aunt, 'I want to go,' and she said okay. When she died later that year, I remember I looked at my reflection in the icebox in the grocery store, and I had black marks under my eyes. Did you ever see shock do that? I looked like I had two black eyes. I went back to live with my mother then. She lived just down the street."

Rutledge attended Courtenay Grammar School, on the corner of Mary and Meeting Streets. It was built in 1885, and his father had gone to school there, too. The original building has long since been demolished and was replaced in the 1950s with a two-story brick structure which is now gone also. The original school had five stories and went from the first grade through seventh grade. There was no middle school back then, and high school started in eighth grade. Rutledge says, "I went to Murray High School. I studied regular courses but they also trained people for jobs. I tried woodshop, auto shop, electrical shop, but didn't like any of them, so I ended up in machine shop. I even took a job in the tool room while I was going to school there. Then I put in an application for the Navy Yard in 1941 and they took me. I worked there until 1943 and went to Merchant Marine school. I served in the war zones and was gone for seven years."

Although Inez grew up in the same neighborhood as Rutledge, her childhood was quite different than his. "My parents were immigrants – from Italy. They came here before I was born. My daddy had a grocery store – the one he sold to Rutledge's daddy when I was a baby. Later, he sold vegetables and fruit from his truck. He used to go to a big produce place in the City Market to get fruit and things and then he would go around and sell it in the street from the truck. He'd drive around town and sometimes I'd sit in the back of it to make sure nobody took anything when he got out to make the delivery. I was only about four or five but I can still remember that. I guess before I was born, he would make deliveries in a horse-drawn wagon because I have a picture of Papa holding my sister on a horse in front of the store. Years later, during the war, he went in his truck to big housing complexes in the north area where people who worked at the shipyard rented. I remember he'd come home with big jars of money! The shipyard really helped the economy at that time. My mama even got a job there during the war. She even wore coveralls!"

Inez says, "We lived at 14 Reid Street all the time I was growing up. We used to go to church at Our Lady of Mercy on America Street. I went to St. Patrick's School on St. Philip Street and walked there every day from Reid Street. Then, when I was sixteen, we moved to a house on the corner of Morris Street and Rutledge Avenue. I was at Bishop England High School at the time. I still have some of the friends I went to high school with."

Inez at The Battery

As for fun, Inez says, "When I was little, I really didn't do much of anything but maybe go to the movies on Saturday and Sunday at the Gloria and the Riviera. I'd just follow my sister around. She didn't like it though because she was five years older. When I was a teenager, I'd walk from Reid Street down to The Battery. It was a real long way but it was just something to do. It was always crowded at The Battery. People were always there so that's where we went. And we always walked." (Rutledge adds that he never rode anywhere until he went to Murray High School and was given a bike to get there.)

When she was in high school, Inez worked at the uptown Woolworth. "They had two Woolworths on King Street - one uptown and one downtown. This one was right by Reid and Ann Streets. After I finished Bishop England, I went to work at Sears Roebuck which was on the corner of King and Calhoun at the time. A little later, in 1950, I went to work for Dr. Warren on Broad Street and that's when I worked with Rutledge's sister. I went to work at the Navy Yard in 1951.

"Back in those days, it seems nobody had anything but they really didn't know there was anything else," Inez says. Rutledge agrees and adds, "Charleston has become one of the most important cities in the country. My son is in the airline business and is always praising it for some reason or another." But Rutledge Cox is still 'old Charleston.' He hates to eat out in restaurants and Inez fixes him Hoppin' John every week or two. He also wants red rice, lima beans on white rice, and baked sweet potatoes - all the old dishes he grew up eating.

In his Charleston brogue, Rutledge says, "My father's first grocery store is gone now but the house I was born in behind it is still there. And the store on the corner of Reid and Drake is also still there but it looks like it could fall down any minute. I don't know what's holding it up. They tore down the one on Blake and America Streets and it was a better building, so I don't know why they tore it down. There is just an empty lot there now."

Empty, but full of memories.

REMEMBERING GOOD TIMES

Betty Ravenel Hennessy

Betty Ravenel Hennessy was an only child, and her parents had been married thirteen years before she came along. "So I was a spoiled brat!" she admits. Of course, that's relative, considering that Charleston was in the throws of the Great Depression when she was growing up. "Nobody had any money. I never got toys in the middle of year – only on Christmas, period - but my mother always saw to it that I had a rubber ball. She'd go to Edward's Five and Dime and get them. We used to play kick ball and dodge ball. I always had the ball, and if I got mad, I'd take the ball and go home. Once a year, the men from the city would come and clean the street drains, and we'd stand around waiting on them to bring up all the rubber balls that had gone down in the drains!"

Betty's father was a city fireman. He worked at the fire station on Cannon Street near King. "I used to go around there and play on the fire engines. There was a red motorcycle with a sidecar and I'd also play on that. He worked 24 hours on, 24 off. He'd get off from work early in the morning, and I'd beg Mama to let me go meet Daddy. I was five years old and would walk up Coming Street by myself to meet him." Betty also remembers her father taking her with him to the Elks Club on Society Street near King Street. "It was strictly men – no women. But Daddy would bring me and sit me up on the bar."

Betty says another perk she had as an only child was that she always got to go to the circus. "My uncle worked at the *News and Courier*, and he got complimentary tickets - the best in the house.

My mother had hay fever and didn't want to be around all that hay at the circus, so I went with my cousin. We'd be right in the front seat. We could see all the shows. A lot of children went to the circus, but they didn't have the seats we did!"

Like most people, Betty always shopped on King Street. "I used to like the Bandbox. I remember taking two or three dresses back to the dressing room to try them on, and Mr. Mendelsohn would bring me another one he thought I might like. I'd tell my mother, 'Oh, I like both of these!' and I'd come out with two dresses!"

Even her family's maid would agree that Betty mostly got what she wanted and ruled the roost. "She came to work for us early in the morning every day and would leave after she bathed me in the afternoon. She would be calling me in to give me by bath so she could go home, and I'd be resisting. She'd say, 'Betty, you is the sick'nin'est child!'"

Betty's maid lived four blocks away on Perry Street. "I'd go over to her house one afternoon a week and play with her little girl. Our house was at 289 Coming Street, between Carolina and Sumter Streets. The house on the corner of Carolina backed up into it and so did the one on the corner of Sumter. There was no yard to it at all. We didn't have a blade of grass! So I had my play area under the house. It was higher than anything in the neighborhood and was the only one built high off the ground. It was all open under there, and I could even stand up in it. There was plenty of room. We kept coal in there, too. There were two doors that opened onto the street, and the coal truck would back up and dump the coal in. It was also the coolest house in the city of Charleston! It was shaped like an 'L' and had fourteen windows downstairs and fourteen upstairs."

Betty's first school was Mrs. Moorer's Kindergarten. "She was on Rutledge Avenue. I remember walking there all by myself! Then

I attended Sacred Heart Catholic School from grades one through six. There were a number of Catholics in my neighborhood, and all my friends were Catholic. My father was a Huguenot but my mother was a Catholic. I am Catholic through-and-through."

Betty remembers playing at Mitchell Playground. "And there was a big field next to where the Greek Church is now on Race Street and we'd play there, too. We used to go everywhere! I'd walk from Coming Street all the way down to The Battery with friends. I wasn't even ten years old! And I could tell you every facet of the old museum on Rutledge Avenue – the leatherback turtle with the bullet hole in it; the whale hanging from the ceiling; the bird eggs."

Betty also remembers going with her parents to the Elks Club beach house on Folly in the early 1930s. "It was right on the front beach. I think it was blown away in a hurricane or maybe it caught fire. But what the Elks had was a big social place, and off to the side were individual rooms where members could stay for a week or whatever. We'd go there and have a grand time. My mother and daddy were party people."

Betty's life changed dramatically when her father died of a heart attack when she was ten years old. "He was laid out at my house but I never saw him. Everything was over when I was allowed to come back home. I thought I was old enough, but they didn't want me there.

"After Daddy died, Mama made our house into two apartments – one on each floor. Mama and I stayed downstairs and rented out the upstairs. A lot of people rented out rooms or parts of their houses in those days. Before Daddy died, we rented out two rooms of our house to girls who came from the country to work at the Cigar Factory. Even when I was grown, my husband and I rented an apartment upstairs in a house on New Street, just below Broad. I remember we paid $40 a month.

"Mama's cousin owned a number of different houses that she rented out. She owned a good bit of property on Spring Street around Kate's Drive-In. She advised my mother to buy the house next door to her house on Calhoun Street. It had a back room off to itself that we could rent out. She told her, 'If you get that house, it's close to the hospitals and the medical college and you'll never have any trouble renting it. So we moved to 238 Calhoun Street.'"

The house on Calhoun was between Smith and Ogier Street, a little street half a block between Smith and Rutledge. "There were very few kids over there – so it was a shock from our previous neighborhood. But my mother made sure I had a bicycle and I used to ride it up to the old neighborhood all the time."

Betty continued to attend school at Sacred Heart after they moved to Calhoun Street. "I'd take a bus up to school every day. I'd get off on the corner of Rutledge and Congress Street and walk over a block to school. Once a week, I took piano lessons after school. The music teacher lived around the corner from school, so I'd walk over to her house and take the bus home after the lesson. One morning when I got up, the weather was not nice – it was a real dark, rainy day. So I asked Mama to please let me cancel my lesson that day and come right home after school. She said all right, so I called the music teacher – Mrs. Moorer - to tell her I was not coming to my music lesson after school. She said, 'Music lesson! I can't even see the cross on the top of Sacred Heart Church – it's gone!' We didn't know it had been hit by a tornado or how bad it was because we were down on Calhoun Street. Father Wolfe, the pastor, was in the rectory at the time and broke his toe. When they fixed it, he always walked with a little limp. But if I hadn't called the music teacher that morning, I'd have gone on up there to school in a tornado!"

When Betty was in the seventh grade, she began attending Bishop England High School. "It only took me five minutes to walk there. There was a group of us who walked home together. The others lived on Bull, Rutledge, and Montagu so I was the first to get out of the crowd. When I got home, Mama always had dinner on the table – the two o'clock dinner.

"We lived within the boundaries of St. Patrick's Church, but my mother had gotten rid of our car when Daddy died and there were no bus routes that ran near St. Patrick's. So we joined St. Mary's Church on Hasell Street. I remember she used to 'buy' her pew. You didn't put money in the collection basket - you paid to have that pew. Boy, she always wanted to sit in her pew! I sang in the choir so I'd be sitting up in the balcony. There were very few children at St. Mary's because there was no school there, but they did have Sunday school for the younger ones. Every year, I had to be with them in the May Procession. Even when I was a big horse in nurses' training, Sister Miriam would call Sister Maria at St. Francis Hospital and say, 'Betty has to be here in the May Procession.' There were three or four of us older girls, and they wanted somebody with a strong voice."

Betty says that, as a teenager, she wasn't allowed to date but could go to dances. "We went out in groups. We had school dances – there was a big one during the May Day celebration every year. And during the war, they had dances on Sunday afternoons at St. Patrick's Church for the service boys. I'd go to those. I remember one time Tommy Dorsey was going to play at a dance at County Hall. Jitterbugging was the thing to do, so I asked my mother if I could go with a boy I knew. My mother was old timey because she was older than all my friends' mothers, and she said, 'Betty, nice girls don't go to public dances.' I begged and begged and, sure enough, I got to go!

"During the war I went to a lot of parties. Miss Jennie Reynolds had the USO dances at the Port of Embarkation – way up there by the air base. They didn't have enough older girls up there because there was another USO in town, so Miss Reynolds was always look-ing for somebody to go up there because it was out in the country. So she had to scrape the bottom of the barrel and get high school girls! She called my mother and said, 'Please let Betty go. I will keep an eye on her and take good care of her.' I was sixteen and LOVED to dance! So, we'd walk over to the Manigault House and they'd put us on an Army bus and take us up to the USO. It was in a little concrete building that was hot as hell in the summertime. Before we left home, we'd put our hair up in curls and have a kerchief tied around it. There was a café called the Air Base Café, and when we drove past that, it was time to take our hair down. We'd go into the dance all dolled up, but within ten minutes, we were drenched! I received a pin showing I had spent 3,000 hours up there dancing! After the dance, the bus would bring us back home - right to our front doors - and would stay there until we went in."

Betty says, "We'd see the same boys there for three or four weeks and then they were shipped out. I still correspond with one of the boys I met. He lives in Connecticut. I met some really

Betty at The Battery

nice boys. The boys would be five deep around the dance floor. Every one of them was from away. It was good for me to be able to talk with and socialize with boys from away. It was very, very broadening. We used to joke because every one of them was from 'just outside of.' Apparently, none of them lived in any cities – it was 'just outside of.' I had a grand time! I am ashamed to say it, but I had a grand time during World War II."

Betty graduated from high school at the age of sixteen. "High school stopped after the eleventh grade. I knew I wanted to be a nurse, but St. Francis Hospital wouldn't let me in their nurses' training until I was seventeen. So I thought I'd just have a year off until then. But my mother said, 'You will not take a year off and sit on your backside! You're going to the College of Charleston.' I had no desire to go, although I was never sorry I did. I was only sixteen and that was too young to be in nursing school anyway."

In those days, residents of the city didn't pay tuition at the College but did have to pay for books and lab fees. Betty says, "The College was smaller and not as spread out as it is now. Green Street, right behind Randolph Hall, was open to traffic. There were no more than a couple hundred students. There were very few boys because so many were off to war. You really can't imagine how few civilian men there were around."

The following year, Betty began the nurses' training program at St. Francis Hospital. "There was no such thing as a BS in nursing. You went for three years and then took the state boards to become a Registered Nurse. My aunt was very friendly with Sister Maria who was in charge of the nurses at St. Francis. She told her that I was planning to go to nurses' training there, and Sister Maria said, 'She'll never make it!' We worked seven days a week! It was during the war and there were very few nurses because so many were in the service.

"After I was there for six weeks, I went to Sister Maria and said, 'I don't have to take all this!' I felt I was always being treated like a slave. But by the end of the month, I got my dander up and vowed they weren't going to run me out. I worked five months in the labor and delivery room – with no days off! There was nobody staffing the night duty except the students. I couldn't sleep during the day and lost weight. These young nurses today can't believe how they used to treat us."

And Betty admits, "I got punished each year I was in nurses' training! One time, I was sneaking to my mother's house in my student nurse's uniform. That was forbidden! We could wear the uniform only at the hospital. I got to the corner and Sister Maria was standing outside the Sisters' home behind the hospital with her hands on her hips motioning for me to come back. I ended up getting restricted for one month and couldn't go out at night."

But Betty adds, "We used to have fun on the first floor with those old men. Sister Perpetua would say, 'Miss Ravenel, stop singing!' or 'Miss Ravenel, stop swinging those hips!' And as long as you had a cleaning cloth in your hand, she was happy."

All of the St. Francis nursing students lived in a huge old house on Ashley Avenue, a block and a half from the hospital. "We lived eight to a room - there were four bunk beds in each room." There was another house for the students on Bennett Street. Nurses-in-training were not allowed to live at home, nor were they allowed to be married.

The medical college didn't offer nurse's training, so girls either attended Roper or St. Francis. Betty explains, "At Roper, they got to see a lot of different kinds of cases. They really got more experience than we did, when you come down to it. They also had psychiatric and pediatric training at Roper, and we didn't have those. We had to go away to Washington, D.C. for three months for that. But I wouldn't give anything for that experience! There was a pediatric hospital in an old section of Washington and a psychiatric hospital outside of Washington. A lot of the rank-and-file as well as service personnel were there."

While she was in training, Betty belonged to the Cadet Nurse Corps. "If you signed up and promised to serve three years in the service after you graduated, they'd give you a stipend and pay for your books. You would go into the service as a regular commissioned officer. I didn't have to serve because the war ended. But I still had all my books paid for, and we got $15 a month spending money. We could do whatever we wanted with it. We used to take it down to the hotels and buy apple swizzles!

"After I had finished my training and taken my state boards, I was sitting on my porch reading one day, and a classmate of mine came by. She said, 'Hey, Rav. Come on and work at Roper. They've got all the clean linen you want.' We used to hoard linen at St. Francis and we had linens that were patched to the hilt. Sister Josephine was head of the laundry. She has a place in heaven! She would be in that hot laundry all day long. I don't believe she weighed a hundred pounds.

"So I got an interview at Roper. Irene Dixon was the head of Roper Hospital at the time. There is a wing at the hospital named for her. She was a friend of my aunt. She told me to come to work Monday morning, and I said, 'I can't come to work on Monday! I am going to New York on vacation next week!' So, I went on my trip, then came home and went to work at Roper. I stayed there two years. My husband was still a student at The Citadel when I finished nurses' training, so we got married when he graduated in 1950." He was a local boy.

Betty remembers, "When I was dating different boys, I'd bring somebody new home for Mama to meet, and she'd sit him down and ask, 'Who was your mother?' The war kind of changed all that. When she was young, people would marry people from their own neighborhoods. She had lived over a store on King Street on the corner of Liberty Street and would talk about going to dances at the medical college and at The Citadel."

Betty's mother's maiden name was Seibert. "One of her ancestors was a tobacco dealer from Cuba. I don't know how far back that was. My grandfather Seibert was a night chemist at the fertilizer factory up on the industrial section of King Street. My grand-mother was a Roses.

"My father's family were Huguenots, but Daddy and his brother both married Catholic girls, so that is how there came to be Catholic Ravenels. My daddy always said he didn't want to live a Catholic but he wanted to die a Catholic - and he did! When I got engaged, I remember one of the relatives from his side coming around to my house and telling me not to ever forget that I had Huguenot blood coursing through my veins. When I was working at the Medical University, I had a friend there whose mother was big in the Huguenot Society. She joined, so I joined also. They'd have talks, and the refreshments were delicious."

When Betty was about twelve, "there were twin Ravenel cousins who came to visit from New York. They were older – nineteen or twenty – and they were darling. They stayed on the eighth floor of the Francis Marion Hotel. It was when Burnett Maybank was sworn in as governor, and there was a parade in Charleston. We had our heads out the window of their room and were throwing confetti and celebrating."

Betty has seen big physical changes to the peninsula over the years. "I remember I was working on the fifth floor of Roper when they were filling all that land around there at the end of Calhoun Street. Barre Street was not even built yet. When they were going to build the Ashley House, they filled it in with refrigerators and every kind of thing they could find. And I remember when they built the Health Department over there after the land was filled in."

Even a few blocks to the east, the area around Betty's house at 238 Calhoun was very low when she lived there. She says, "Every time it would rain, it would flood under our house. We had a cistern under there. The house would be sitting on that water for weeks, but we never had a termite or anything! Amazing. You couldn't put a nail in that wood, it was so hard. Putting up curtain rods and all was very difficult."

Betty's house on Calhoun Street is gone now. She remembers, "There were also two nice houses on the corners of Smith Street and Calhoun. They had cupolas and round rooms and lots of gingerbread on them. One was on the lot where Stuhr's Funeral Home is now. It was a fraternity house for students from the medical college. On the other corner is where Dr. Pat Carter's mother lived. I used to see her passing by my house when she was walking back and forth to medical school." A laundry is on that corner now.

In addition to seeing houses disappear, Betty has also seen some local traditions fade away. "At four o'clock every afternoon, my cousin and my aunt and uncle and my mother's cousin would come by in the car and 'toot-toot-toot-toot' and we'd come out for a ride around the city. We'd drive around The Battery and my mother would be saying, 'So-and-so lived in that house, and so-and-so lived in that one.' I was a child and could've cared less! But sometimes we'd stop at McKay's Drug Store for a milkshake. It was across from Condon's Department Store on King Street. You'd park at an angle and a boy would come out and take your order." Many older Charlestonians will tell you that taking a ride around town was an important daily ritual. But Betty adds, "Sometimes we'd drive cross the Ashley River. It was all farms out there. Or we'd ride to see my aunt in Meggett or ride to the island" (Sullivan's).

Betty remembers another tradition. "When I was a teenager, people would walk on King Street after the stores closed. We'd buy a soda at Frierson's or Duffy's Pharmacy. Then we'd walk to Devotions at St. Mary's Church. They'd have Devotions every evening. The church was an integral part of our lives."

Another faded memory was that "we used to have dances on the beach in the summertime on Folly. And the Knights of Columbus took up a lot of our time as young adults. We'd have the annual Labor Day picnics at Alhambra Hall in Mt. Pleasant. Afterward, we'd take home what was left, and people would come by and we'd all party the rest of the night! The 'KC' used to have dances, too. My husband was in the Fourth Degree, and everything they had was formal. I remember his first formal. We were just married and didn't have any money, so Jimmy McAlister told my husband, 'Come on down to the funeral home and I'll loan you a tux.' Years later, he bought his first one from Johnny Morris at Kessler's on King Street."

One thing about Charleston that hasn't changed is the importance of friendship. "The friends I've had all my life were friends from the beginning. A few of us couples played poker once a month for forty years! And, as many months as we can, several of my girl-friends and I still go to lunch.

"It's just like when we were in school."

OUTLINING HISTORY

Lewis Bowen

Like so many people who grew up in Charleston during the first half of the 20th century, Lewis Bowen no longer lives downtown. But in his suburban home, he is surrounded by plenty of visual reminders of the Holy City. "When I retired in 1996, I started making silhouettes of Charleston scenes for family and friends. First, I take a photograph of something; then I draw a picture of it and make a stencil or template. I secure that to an eighth-inch piece of Baltic birch wood and cut it out." Lewis has a silhouette of the old Cooper River Bridge and the Ravenel Bridge, the steps at High Battery, several different churches, and horse-drawn carriages. He even has some depicting historical events, such as the Citadel cadets firing on the *Star of the West* just before the Civil War. There is one of a shrimp boat at Shem Creek, the McCloud Plantation house, and of course, the Angel Oak. He points to a silhouette with an intricate design - a gate at the College of Charleston. "It takes about 45 hours to do that one." He shows another of a gate at The Citadel but admits, "The sword gates on Legare Street are one of my favorites." Lewis says he has about 250 different designs. "I used to do the weekly farmers' market at Marion Square but I'm getting too old for it now, so I mainly sell at craft shows."

Lewis and his twin brother George were born in Charleston in 1928 and spent much of their youth living on George Street in Ansonborough. Lewis describes their street. "My dad had a shop, Southern Welding Works, on the corner of George and Anson Street, and we lived opposite it. From our house down to the corner of Anson, there was a lumber yard. We used to enjoy watching all

Lewis (right) and his twin brother up on the roof

the activity going on there." The family moved to 217 Rutledge Avenue for a brief time, then back to George Street in 1932. He says, "All that part of George is torn down now. Our second house is still standing, but the first house we lived in is gone."

That house is at 3 George Street and is a two-story 'Charleston single house' with an attic floor and two large side porches. Lewis says, "We had two huge pecan trees in the yard with swings hanging from them. When we were little, my mother would take us up to the attic and put us out on the roof of the porch to pick up pecans that had fallen into the gutter. She didn't want to waste them! But she also didn't want us to fall off the roof, so she would tie a sheet around our waists.

"The house is a painted wooden house, and my twin brother must've thought the paint tasted good because he ate a lot of it and got lead poisoning. He was sick in bed for a while. Dr. Banov from the health department came to the house. I remember we also used to go to his office on Wentworth Street and get shots. Dr. Banov would go to schools to give shots, too. They were pretty good about that."

Lewis attended Bennett Grammar School on the corner of St. Philip and George Streets, across from the College of Charleston. "We used to walk back and forth every day. It was only two and a half blocks from our house - a straight shot across Meeting and King Streets. Bennett was a stucco building – gray. I remember my first grade teacher, Mrs. Robinson. She took us on field trips. One

I remember was to the airport, and we went inside an airplane there. In our classroom, we had a model of an airplane that we could get in. One time, we all had to build a small airplane out of wood. When I brought it home, I took it up to the second floor and dropped it. It went straight down!"

Lewis remembers as a child going to the swimming pool at the YMCA on George Street. "We also went swimming at the municipal pool which was right across the street from our house. That was a huge pool, and we had a lot of fun. They had a ten-foot diving board!" The pool sat back about a hundred yards off the street, next to a mansion that was used as the offices for the water works and is now the headquarters for Spoleto USA.

Another mansion Lewis remembers from his Ansonborough neighborhood was on the corner of Meeting and George Streets. "It was a beautiful home. It was quite large and very ornate. They tore it down and now there is a little brick building there. Across from it, on the southeast corner of George, was an Esso station – Lillienthal's."

There are a few other images Lewis remembers from his neighborhood. "There used to be some people living down George Street who would carry a canoe on their heads and walk it down to the river." He also remembers the ice man coming through in a horse-drawn wagon. "He'd chip off twenty-five pounds or whatever we needed and he'd put it in a case. He'd carry it over his shoulder into our kitchen and put it in the ice box. We'd stand in back of his wagon and wait on him to come back out, and he'd give us shavings of ice. That was a treat! Also I remember the vegetable wagon used to come by. A two-wheel wagon that he'd pull or push. And I will always remember the shrimp man and fish man hollering as they came through."

Lewis explains, "We used to eat a lot of vegetables and a lot of fish and shrimp. And grits and rice. My mother was a great cook.

She used to make a lot of tea cakes – little cookies, really. We loved those! And every Christmas, she used to bake a fruitcake and wrap it in a cloth."

Sometimes, the family would eat out at Robertson's Cafeteria on Broad Street. "We used to eat there mostly on Sunday. And next to it was an ice cream parlor. We used to get a double dip of ice cream. That was a real treat! We thought it cost a lot of money."

Lewis's mother cooked every day, but she had some help with the laundry. "We had a black lady who came to the house and she used to build a fire in the back yard. She'd put a big pot over the fire and put lye in it for cleaning the clothes. She used a stick to punch them around. Then she rinsed them and would hang them on the line." One of Lewis's wooden silhouettes depicts the scene.

Lewis and his family attended Citadel Square Baptist Church on Meeting Street. "We used to walk to church. We'd go every Wednesday night and every Sunday. When I was very young - I may have been six years old – Dr. Pettigrew was the pastor. When I was ten, I was baptized and joined the church. My oldest brother, Ward, taught Sunday school classes for many years on the radio. He taught the men's class in the church's auditorium, and the radio station would broadcast the lesson."

Lewis still has the little suit he wore in his brother's wedding at their church. It is in mint condition. "I was two years old at the time. My twin brother and I came a long time after the first four boys and my sister. We were latecomers."

Lewis's oldest brother and his father owned the welding company together. "They did welding and repairs on tanks that gas and fuel oil are kept in. First, they'd send the tanks down to Southern Ice Company on Market Street to have them steamed out so they could get into the tank and repair and weld it. In 1931, one of my brothers was welding inside a tank and he was electrocuted. I was only three at the time but I remember him. He used to play with my twin brother and me on the floor of our house. I also remember he used to play on Charleston High School's football team and we'd go to the games."

Lewis remembers a few other things about having older brothers. "When we lived on Rutledge Avenue, we had kind of a barn in the back of the lot. Inside, there was a big opening at the top and a ladder going up to it. When my twin brother and I were very little, my older brothers would drop us down from up top to the brothers below who would catch us! I also remember in the evening, we'd sit out on the side porch. We had swings and rocking chairs out there – it was quite a nice memory. We had cans that we'd put rags in and we lit the rags so they'd smolder to keep the mosquitoes away. And a couple times a week, all our family would get together in the evening and have a bible reading." Lewis also remembers the family singing around their player piano. "I took piano lessons from Vernon Westin who was the organist and choir director from our church."

Like most kids who grew up when Lewis did, "we'd get in the street and play. And I used to go fishing at The Battery. Once I caught a big turtle but I couldn't get him up because he was so heavy. And there was a basketball net outside Bennett School so we played there a lot. The school playground was all dirt. We also used to go to the Green in front of the old Citadel and have pick-up football games. One of my older brothers was in the National Guard and we used to watch them march on the Green, too."

Lewis and his twin brother attended Bennett School through the sixth grade. Then in 1940, his family moved out to Dupont Road (now Stinson Road), West of the Ashley. "There is a store on that corner of Savannah Highway that sells tire rims. Our house was on that corner. We had about three quarters of an acre, all the way back to the railroad track. And we had a huge oak tree in the yard.

"The road went back into Edmond Bellinger's farm. There used to be nothing but the farm back there. Later, Mr. Truluck had an airport on a portion of the farm. They kept crop dusters back there and they also gave flying lessons. We used to go hunting back there and we'd bring back rabbits and squirrels. My mother would make rabbit salad - like chicken salad. We also had a lot of chickens in our yard and I remember having to kill the chickens by twirling them around by the neck.

"When I was about twelve, I worked picking up cabbage and potatoes at Bellinger's. I'd drive the truck from his farm up to the produce market on the corner of Wappoo Road, across Savannah Highway. They also used to hook up a horse and wagon and we'd drive around with him and sell vegetables in neighborhoods like Edgewater Park."

At that age, Lewis and his brother were in the Boy Scouts. "We rode our bikes from our house on Savannah Highway all the way out to the Boy Scout camp on Wadmalaw Island. It was a long ride! We were going camping and did that for our merit badge. Every night out there, we used to have a circle and I was introduced to the Order of the Arrow. The ones in charge would come around and knock you out of the circle. It was a pretty sudden blow – you didn't know what hit you – but it was supposed to be an honor. Come to find out, I was blindfolded and led into the woods. I had to stay out in the woods alone all night and find my way back to camp the next morning! Once I got back, I couldn't talk to anyone for the whole day. I had to work all day, and finally they gave us a meal that night. The biggest thing I remember getting out of it was a sash with a large arrow. I wore it over my uniform."

Lewis has a photograph of himself and his twin brother when they were in scouts. "We used to come to the meetings downtown at Citadel Square Church. We took a bus in from West Ashley and got off at Marion Square and walked over. On occasion, we might leave something on the bus. The bus went down to Wentworth Street and back up Rutledge Avenue, so we'd run over there to meet it and get our stuff off the bus, then run back to the church for the meeting."

Eventually, Lewis and his family changed churches. "My dad was instrumental in getting Ashley River Baptist Church started. Everything over there was just cabbage fields at the time, and we took turns having services in the homes of the dozen or so members. Finally, we had enough money to build the church where it is now - next to St. Andrew's Shopping Center."

Lewis and his brother attended St. Andrew's High School starting in the seventh grade. Later, while he was still a student there, he used to drive the school bus. "I used to pick up the kids in the morning and take them home afterward. I got $25 a month for doing it." Lewis also drove the football team when they had 'away' games. "I even drove the bus over the very narrow old Cooper River Bridge when I'd take the team over to play against Moultrie High School."

Lewis was very active in sports during high school. He has a composition book in which he has pasted old newspaper photos of his various teams. "My brother and I both played football. I played four years - quarterback and end." In the composition book, there are also newspaper articles from 1943 to 1947 announcing when every game would be played as well as the results afterward. He also played basketball and has the mimeographed basketball schedules for each season. The St. Andrew's Rocks played Murray, Bishop England, North Charleston, Porter, College Prep, Chicora, and Charleston High. He has written in the final scores of each game. In a photograph of the basketball team, Lewis points out himself and his twin brother. Lewis is holding the team trophy. "I was center on the basketball team. In this picture, our coach was Corky Griffith. Jack Simmons was our first coach. He'd played football at The Citadel."

Lewis still has one of his high school letters for his participation in sports. Another that he has belongs to his wife. "She was a cheerleader at St. Andrew's. We met in high school."

Lewis's scrapbooks are personal keepsakes of his own life's history. His silhouettes are reminders of Charleston's.

Note: A new memento Lewis has just added to his scrapbook is a newspaper clipping from December 12, 2012. He exclaims, "After 84 years, I made my first hole-in-one at Shadowmoss Golf Course!"

SCHOOL DAYS, SCHOOL DAYS

Virginia (Ginny) Blank Bowen

Ginny Blank Bowen remembers being very busy with extra-curricular activities when she was a student at St. Andrew's High School in the 1940s. She was a cheerleader for the football and basketball teams, and preparing for the spring musicals was also a big commitment. "We began practicing in October for the May performances!"

Before attending St. Andrew's, Ginny went to the private Ashley Hall girls' school for two years. "My mother had gone to Ashley Hall and wanted me to go. I had friends there but I didn't really want to go to an all-girls school. And I wanted one that had its own sports programs."

At Ashley Hall, Ginny was a cheerleader for the all-male Porter Military Academy. "Porter was right around the corner from Ashley Hall, and they were always pushing the two schools together. We dated Porter cadets, and the captains of their football teams chose the cheerleaders. Somebody told me my picture is hanging in Porter-Gaud School," she says.

Porter's campus was on the corner of Ashley Avenue and Bee Street. Two of the old school's buildings are still standing – St. Luke's Chapel and Waring Library - and are now part of the MUSC campus. "My youngest brother went to Porter when it was there. At that time, the Porter boys wore military-style uniforms."

Porter has since moved, but Ashley Hall is still in its original location. The girls' school ran from kindergarten through twelfth grade, as it does today. When Ginny attended, there were a lot of boarding students in the high school program. "It was about half and half. Former First Lady Barbara Bush was there, but that was before I was there. We invited two of the boarding students to have Thanksgiving with us and one had Christmas with us. Their fathers gave them a credit card and told them to go buy us all these gifts, but my mother didn't want them to do that. I didn't either; we were just being friendly."

Ginny's father had insisted that she attend Ashley Hall for at least two years. Ginny was allowed to transfer to St. Andrew's for the remaining three years of high school. "We had a wonderful principal at St. Andrew's - Mr. Hester. My high school years there were wonderful. I enjoyed everything about them. Every time we've had a reunion, I've been."

When she was very young, Ginny's family lived downtown, so she started first grade at Craft Grammar School. "But you couldn't start if you weren't six by September. They had half-years then, so I started school in the middle of the year. Christmas had just passed, and the worst thing when I started school was that some of the children told me there was no Santa Claus! Mama was very upset.

"At the time, we were living on Queen Street, so I was able to walk to school at Craft. Then, we moved to a big house on the corner of Bull and Rutledge and lived in an apartment there. The museum was right there. It was creepy but it was so much fun! I remember the old rickety steps and the dark room with stars. And they had costumes from all the wars and wax figures of Indians. It was interesting to see. That building was magical – the creeky boards and all. I loved the museum!"

Ginny remembers they were living in the house on that corner when the tornado hit Charleston in 1938. "It was a stormy day and

I didn't go to school that day. Oh my gosh - you could hear the Market collapsing! I was standing in the kitchen and holding my baby sister while my mother was washing dishes. She dropped a dish and said she was glad I was holding the baby because she said she probably would've dropped her! Afterward, people were out on the streets talking and the town was all black – the electricity was out. My daddy was out of town with his job and he tried to call us through the Red Cross. They told him nothing was standing in Charleston - they said Charleston was flat and that there were very few people alive! Mama was finally able to call him and he was so glad to hear we were okay. We were on the same circuit as St. Francis Hospital, so once they got the generators operating, we even had lights."

Ginny's family moved to Stocker Drive, West of the Ashley, when she was nine. She then attended St. Andrew's Elementary. "Almost everything around us was woods back then, but they did have tennis courts in Windermere on the corner of Savannah Highway. We mainly played in the neighborhood. We played kickball and skated in the streets. We played 'Pop the Whip' on Highway 17 - can you imagine! But, by the time I was a teenager, James Island was being built up and the Navy Yard traffic was beginning - bumper to bumper! When I was married and had kids, I would've liked to buy my mother's house on Stocker Drive, but the traffic was too bad by then."

When Ginny was born, her parents were living in Hendersonville, North Carolina. Her mother's family had moved there because her grandfather had TB, "and the doctors wanted him out of this climate in Charleston. They used to go up there during the summers anyway, so they decided to go and live up there for a couple years. My parents met up there – my daddy was from Virginia. But when I was a year old, it was the Depression. Daddy lost his job up there and Grandmamma lost her job as bookkeeper at the Hendersonville Hotel, so we came back to Charleston to be with family.

"My granddaddy's brothers, the Ostendorffs, owned the Cadillac dealership off Meeting Street near the Market. But my granddaddy didn't work a whole lot. Sometimes he used to go there, but Grandmamma had to work because my granddaddy didn't. He used to take care of me a lot. He was real good. He'd take me on the bus to Hampton Park, and he'd take me fishing. They used to have fishing contests at Colonial Lake. One time I caught two fish on the hook at the same time. I won a rod and reel and a pair of shorts! The Sportsman Shop sponsored the tournament."

Ginny at Hampton Park

Ginny explains, "When we moved from Hendersonville, we all lived in the same house because nobody had any money. It was near Colonial Lake. But we didn't live there long - just long enough to get settled and for Daddy to get a job. Grandmamma got a job as a court stenographer and my daddy went to work for C.D. Franke wholesalers. Then my parents and I moved to Water Street. The house had two apartments in it and we rented one. From there, we moved to Queen Street into an apartment in a big house they've torn down now. It was in the middle of the next block up from Craft School," where part of the Robert Mills Housing Project is today.

After they left the house by the lake, Ginny's grandparents moved to Glebe Street. They lived there for a long time in the upstairs apartment of one of the brick single houses that are now part of the College of Charleston campus. Ginny's grandmother was a member of nearby Grace Episcopal Church. Ginny says, "I went to kindergarten there. It was called the Grace Little School. I also went to Sunday school and was confirmed there. When I was a teenager, a friend and I taught Sunday school for the little ones. We had a good time at Grace and had a good League (youth group). My husband and I were married at Grace." He was a Baptist, so as a compromise, they began attending John Wesley Methodist Church together. "My grandmother got upset. She said, 'Once an Episcopalian, always an Episcopalian. You can go wherever you want, but you will always be an Episcopalian.'"

When she was a child, Ginny would go to Kanuga, the Episcopal summer camp in Hendersonville. She also frequently went to Girl Scout camp. "Camp Agnes Ann was on the way to Walterboro. We had a good time out there. We slept in cabins, and they had a place you could swim. We had a great scout leader who lived on the water in Edgewater Park. We'd swim off their dock. Her husband owned a dredging company. She was the best! And all the girls went to school together at St. Andrew's grammar school."

Ginny remembers going with her parents out to the country – Yonge's Island - to visit her cousin, Virginia Mixson Gerrity, who became a local expert and pioneer in preserving the Gullah language. "We went down there a lot." Closer to home, "Mama and Daddy took us to The Battery a lot at night because it was hot. We'd go get ice cream from the ice cream parlor on Broad Street. And we also went to the beach - Folly mostly. You could drive on the beach then. I remember dances out there at the Rainbow Corner and also at the Isle of Palms at the end of the pavilion on the front beach. They'd bring a band in every summer. They played every weekend. They had the best band – Mel Felton! That was a lot of fun."

Dancing was a big part of the social scene in Charleston. "In the late 1940s, when I was at St. Andrew's High School, I was invited to a few of the hops at The Citadel. One year, Tommy Dorsey played at the ring hop. They had the dances at the Citadel's gym." Ginny also remembers going to a few USO dances downtown when she was in high school. The dances were well-chaperoned. "There was a building next to the Y on George Street, near the municipal swimming pool, but it's torn down now."

During the war, Ginny's father was an air raid warden for their Stocker Drive neighborhood. "And I remember the POW camp that was in Moreland. They also kept prisoners where the parking lot is now for John Wesley Methodist Church on Highway 17. The church wasn't there at the time. They used to drive the prisoners in trucks down my street taking them to do work or something. We'd stand there on the street and watch them go by. The German prisoners would throw notes at us - written in German. They also had some prisoners that were Italian."

Ginny remembers that, when they lived on Stocker Drive, her mother had a full-time maid. She says, "My mother always had help because daddy traveled so much and she had four kids." When Ginny herself became a mother of four, her mother's maid came to help twice a week. "Our maid was a wonderful cook. She was so good to me and my children. She'd cook supper for us before she went home in the afternoon – shrimp pie and red rice – and a huge apple pie from scratch. She worked for us for about ten years. I was devastated when she left to go live in Washington, D.C. Her brother owned a restaurant up there, and he'd been trying to get her to come work for him for years. Finally, when her son finished high school, she went."

The Civil Rights movement was in its infancy when Ginny's own children were young. She says she doesn't remember there being any big problems during the period, but that's not to say the changes were seamless. "I was the PTA membership chairman when they integrated the elementary school, and I couldn't get all the white parents to join the PTA. Many were upset that they'd integrated, so they boycotted the PTA. When I called them about helping with the school carnival, they refused to help. I explained to them they were backing out on their own children, but I still had a hard time getting people. It wasn't the children – it was the parents. That was probably about 1957 or '58. After a year or so, they were all right."

Another change Ginny has witnessed is a shift in the economic demographics of the city. "When I was a young bride in the early 1950s, I worked at C&S Bank on King Street and handled checking accounts. Many of the people who lived downtown in old homes took in boarders. They had inherited the houses but they didn't have money. There wasn't a lot of money in Charleston."

Ginny adds, "But there's money now."

USED TO BE

Ralph McLaughlin

Ask Ralph McLaughlin what he did growing up in Charleston in the 1930s, and he'll tell you, "I used to swim everywhere. We'd just go out and jump off the docks at the yacht basin by Calhoun Street. We'd just go – nobody to stop us." Calhoun Street ended about where Roper Hospital is now and a creek went out from there into the Ashley River. Lockwood Drive wasn't there - that was all marsh - and the Ashley House (apartment building) had not been built yet. "The lake that is by it was where the old yacht basin was. We'd just jump in there and swim out through the creek to the river.

"I remember when they started filling all that in. Before that, the mine craft base was where the City Marina is now. My daddy was a plumber and we did contract work down there during the Second World War. We put filling stations in there. That three-story building (the old rice mill) was an officers' club. We had our wedding reception there."

Ralph shows off a photograph circa 1960 showing him with his wife in their wooden motorboat at the old yacht basin. Boats have always played a big role in Ralph's life. "I belonged to the Charleston Yacht Club. As teenagers, we'd have a regatta which would run Thursday through Saturday. Then they'd have dances and things after the races. There were three boating clubs around here – the Carolina Yacht Club on East Bay Street, the Mt. Pleasant Yacht Club, and mine. At first, ours was where Halsey Boat Yard

Ralph and his wife Jean at the old yacht basin

was – about where Halsey Street is now – and the headquarters was in what we called the old horse stable. After they paved the road (Lockwood Drive) through, we moved over to where the City Marina is now."

Ralph says much of the city is built on filled-in marshland. He heard older folks say that, when the Francis Marion Hotel was built in the 1920s, "they lost a piling when it was pushed down because the land below it was hollow. It had been marsh originally and it was just landfill.

"Also from South Battery on over to the west, they just kept extending the city," Ralph explains. Back in his mother's day, kids would go swimming off the area that is now Murray Boulevard, or "Low Battery," near where the Ft. Sumter House (formerly hotel) was later built. "She and her friends used to go to the mudflats where the road is built around The Battery. I used to have a picture of my mother and her friend sitting on a pile driver that drove the posts for The Battery's wall. After the sea wall was completed and the marsh dried up, they filled it all in and made Murray Boulevard and South Battery. They used dredged up stuff but there were also two incinerators to burn trash, and they dumped that in the low lying areas to fill it in."

Ralph was born at home, at 30 Magazine Street, across from the old City Jail. "They put the project (Robert Mills Manor) there in 1938, so our house is gone now. When I was a kid living across the street, the jail was still being used. I wasn't afraid of it – I was raised there, so it was just normal to me. The jail's property ran from the corner of Wilson and Magazine Streets up a block and a half or so. Some of that is gone now and an empty lot is there. The street curved around and went down Franklin Street, and the Jenkins Orphanage was there in the old Marine Hospital. Then you'd go down to the corner of Queen Street and there was the medical college – before they tore it down and moved over to Calhoun Street. It was a good size – two story – probably 60 feet wide and 100 feet long. And next to that on Queen Street was the first Roper Hospital. There was a lot of activity in our area with the hospitals and the jail and the orphanage."

Ralph remembers, "The Jenkins Orphanage kids used to go around the streets and play music. I had a picture one time of the kids playing in front of the Orphanage and a lot of women out there dancing 'the Charleston.' One night when I was eight years old, the fire alarms broke out and they sent all the fire departments around there. They had a fire and all of the young boys were jumping out the windows. Nobody was killed and the fire engines put it out.

"My grandmother had land on Franklin Street on the other side of Jenkins Orphanage. She also had land on the side of her house on

Magazine Street. She had cows and chickens, geese, turkeys and all kind of stuff. She used to send out dairy. My aunts and uncles used to deliver milk in the morning. There used to be the milk boat that would come in at the Ft. Sumter Hotel dock so they'd also pick up extra milk that was brought in from a dairy farm over on James Island. Then they'd take it out and deliver it - in cans. My grandmother also had a little store that used to sell meats and sugar, rice and so forth. She used to take in vegetables from the men who came around in pushcarts and sell that off in the shop also. She had an icebox in the store about 10 feet tall, and the ice man would come around every day or two with a 300 pound block of ice and shove it up in there to keep the stuff in the ice box cold."

Ralph's mother's family was German. "Their name was Behlmer. She had three brothers that were machinists. They worked at the Dry Dock on the Cooper River. One of them taught at Murray (Vocational) High School. My father's side was Irish. They came here a long time ago. I don't remember the date but you can go up to St. Lawrence Cemetery and see the name on the gravestone for Matthew McLaughlin, my great-grandfather. My father grew up in Ansonborough in a big twelve-room house on Wentworth Street. Some of his people owned places at 22, 24 and 26 Wentworth. Around the corner from those houses, on Anson Street, was my daddy's plumbing shop.

"That section where my daddy's people lived, Ansonborough, was mostly Catholic. There was St. Joseph's Church, where my parents were married. And St. Mary's Church on Hasell Street and then there was St. Peter's on Wentworth for black Catholics. All of my mother's family was Lutheran. They went to St. Matthew's Church across from The Green (Marion Square). My grandmother was a Bullwinkle before she married Behlmer."

Ralph's mother and his uncles were all born in the same house where he was born – 30 Magazine Street. His mother had attended

Craft School just around the corner. "My cousins on Savage Street (George and Billy Behlmer) were older than us and they went to Craft School, so my oldest brother went there, too. But then Father May came and wanted to know why we were going to a public school when there was a Catholic school a half block down that street. So my daddy sent the other three of us to Cathedral School."

As a plumber many years later, Ralph became aware of something about the Cathedral that even very few Catholics knew about – there was special plumbing system leading from the sacristy of the church upstairs all the way down to Legare Street. "The nuns used to come over and wash the vestments and chalices, and that water couldn't go in with anything else. It had to drain down by itself and go right into the earth." Those were the days of the old traditions of the Catholic Church, the days when eating meat was forbidden on Fridays. "Every Friday morning, when we were living on Magazine Street, the man with the pushcart would come and ring the bell and you could buy any kind of fish or shrimp or crab. So you didn't have to worry about what to fix for dinner!"

Ralph and his family moved to 55 Smith Street when he was ten years old. "They were going to build the housing project and bought our house from us. When we moved, that was like moving to another world. My whole life had been on Magazine Street up until then. But on Smith Street, the black folks used to be right protective of me because they knew my grandmother from her store. If I was riding my bicycle in the street, they'd tell each other, 'Dat Behlmer boy.'"

Ralph attended Charleston High School when it was an all-boys school. "They had about 300 boys there at the time. We had Protestants, Catholics, Greeks, Jews – a mixture. Everybody got along fine. I finished in 1945. Then I went into the plumbing business with my daddy. I had worked with my daddy from the time I was eight years old, but I learned the trade from his hired plumbers.

"We lived on Smith Street through the time I was in high school. My parents had bought that house from the Coca-Cola man – McDowell. He had the Coca-Cola factory on the corner of Meeting and Calhoun Streets. I remember there were horse troughs outside the plant. Horses were used a lot for deliveries. My daddy's plumbing business had supplies delivered to us from the railroad depot by horse and dray (wagon)."

The Coca-Cola plant is long gone and there has been a hotel on that site for decades. Ralph remembers a number of other businesses that are no longer around. "On the waterfront – the Cooper River – was Etiwan Fertilizer Company. The Clyde Line used to pull in at a dock over there also. It would come from New York and was a passenger line but would also bring in all kinds of stuff – including plumbing supplies that we ordered. There was also a coal yard at the foot of Laurens Street (where Dockside Condominiums are now). It was a big company. Further up the waterfront, the same company sold oil and wood. It was hit hard with the big storm of 1938. I was ten years old. That was a bad storm." Ralph remembers, "The water came up above Tradd Street."

On the Ashley River side of the city, Ralph remembers Anderson Lumber Mill on Broad Street near where Lockwood Drive is today and also Halsey Lumber Company on what is now Halsey Street. "They used to float logs down the Wappoo Cut and bring them over to the city to cut them into lumber. They used to bring them up into the marsh" where Lockwood Drive is now.

Ralph remembers when Maybank Highway was built on James Island. "My uncle was the clerk of court. He came and got me and we went across the Wappoo Bridge and went on the new highway all the way to the Stono River – way out there. There was a big celebration. I also remember being in front of the newspaper building across from Gibbes Art Gallery when Maybank was elected governor. There was a lot of excitement then, too."

And, of course, anybody that was around in 1938 remembers the excitement when President Franklin Roosevelt came to the city. "Jerry Lockwood brought him right up to the waterfront on a tugboat, right up to the dock. There was a gang of people there watching." Ralph was ten years old at the time, and it made a big impression on him.

Another childhood memory Ralph shares is how he and his friend used to go to the plumbing shop owned by the friend's grandfather, Julian Smith, at 91 Broad Street and "venture up to the third floor and play. Sometimes we'd climb out onto the roof and walk all the way to the post office along on other rooftops. We could run the whole way. It was a lot of fun! The houses were close enough that we could just walk from one to the other - we usually didn't even have to hop over." He says the roofs were metal but they had on tennis shoes, so walking on the hot tin roofs wasn't a problem. "We'd also pick the time of day."

The yard behind Smith's shop provided more adventure. "We used to go in the back and we'd dig holes and make caves in the yard. We'd even make smoke stacks and have fires in the caves with smoke coming up through them. Over on King Street near Broad, they were going to build houses, and we'd take old man Smith's tools and take the lumber from there and build forts."

On Ralph's wall hangs a framed print by the local artist, Jim Booth, of the view looking north on King Street near Market Street, circa 1900. A street car runs on the track down the middle of the street. The facades of many of the buildings on each side are visible. "When I was coming up, they had the street car coming down King but they had cars parking on the side. A lot of stuff looked the same, though, when I was born 28 years after this." He points out the various buildings in the picture. "Siegling's Music Store was on the corner of Beaufain where the nuns have a store now. You can see there were two big clock towers on King Street on each side of Woolworth. There was a dentist office next to one. My daddy went to him." Ralph points to a beautiful building on the corner of Wentworth. The picture shows it had huge columns and a gold dome roof. "It was called the Emporium. It was open on the bottom level and there were tables in there where they sold all kinds of things. They took it down in the 1930s and put a new Lerner Shop on that corner. Walgreen's was across on the east corner, and later, the power company had a showroom of appliances on that corner."

Ralph also points out where Efird's, Hunley's Drug Store, and Globe Shoe Store were. "On the east side of King Street was Charleston Dry Goods. M.H Lazarus Hardware was on the corner of Hasell. McIntosh was another place. They sold plants and fertilizer. And Frierson's Drug Store was the hangout for kids in high school. They had a soda fountain."

In the lower right corner of the picture is a cigar store. Ralph says, "There were a lot of stores that sold cigars because they made them right here in Charleston. The Cigar Factory made more cigars here than any other cigar factory in the world! One kind was El Roy Tan. My friend was a supervisor there. He'd bring cigars out sometimes and give them to us at the Knights of Columbus."

Another big employer in Charleston was the Dry Dock at the foot of Calhoun Street on the Cooper River. "They always did a lot of work down there, but when the war came, they started making all kinds of ships around here. Then they started building big things up at the Navy Yard in North Charleston. They built many destroyers up there. That was one of the outstanding things they did."

Another print hanging on the wall sparks Ralph's memory of a different section of the city. "Here is Rainbow Row. Up at the north end of Rainbow Row, near the corner of Elliott Street, was a store run by people named Guida. People from the ships would come in and buy tobacco and other things from there. The name is still on the building near the roof line. Down on the other end, the south end of Rainbow Row on the corner of Tradd Street, some of my mother's family ran a grocery store. They lived above the store. It was named Wohler's, and they ran it for a long, long time. When my grandmother's aunt died, she left my mother her furniture. So we inherited something from Rainbow Row! When I had my own plumbing business, I remodeled a lot of those places from the second floor up. I did a big job for a doctor at the eye clinic at the Medical University. It was in the 1970s or 80s, when people were first fixing them up. You ought to see the gardens behind some of these places nowadays! They are beautiful."

But the area wasn't always so pretty. In Ralph's youth, "it was a wreck! My daddy's plumbing business used to hire a lot of black people who lived in there. There was one big strapping man who worked for my daddy, and he lived in there. Sometime, I'd go there to get him when they needed him to work as a day laborer."

Throughout his life, Ralph has had several close acquaintances in the black community. "I've known the Fieldings all my life. They were a family of undertakers and had their business right around the corner from where we lived on Magazine Street. It was on the corner of Logan and Short Street; then they moved farther up Logan, which is where they are now. Herbert Fielding became a senator."

Ralph considered the prominent African-American blacksmith, Philip Simmons, a friend. "When Philip was young, he lived on Daniel Island and helped with his family farm. When he was four-teen, he decided he was going to venture into Charleston to see what else he could get into. He started working with his uncle and made wagon wheels. Then he went into being a blacksmith. When I had my plumbing business, I would take tools to Philip, and he'd sharpen them up. He did that for many people. And I used to go to his house on Blake Street and do whatever I could to help him. He started off his shop down on Laurens Street, right by my uncle Freddie Behlmer's machinist's shop. Then he started making drawings of gates and got into making gates all over the city. He made over 500 gates! The first gate he made was for Jack Krawcheck on King Street." Ralph shows off a framed photo of Simmons working at the anvil. "I treasure this picture. It was taken at the park where the old museum was (Cannon Park). One time, there was a celebration down there and he was making things. You can see my wife in the picture too. He was a wonderful friend."

It's no secret that Charleston has become a mecca for transplanted residents and it's harder and harder to run across life-long residents like Ralph. But he shares an amusing story illustrating how small the world really still is. "One night years ago, my wife and I were sitting on the rail at The Battery. A couple walked past and remarked, 'It sure is nice in Charleston.' They told us they were visiting from Georgia. The woman said, 'I've never lived here, but I have some relatives here that tell me all about it.' So I asked the woman, 'Who is your family?' She replied that it was Billy Behlmer. I told her, 'Then you're my cousin!'"

Ralph McLaughlin has witnessed the city's many changes over the last eighty-plus years. Its physical size has increased due to the filling in of land he once knew as creeks and marshes. The construction of new buildings in those areas and the conversion of many older homes to condos has been another change. And, of course, Ralph can tell you about all the buildings that are no longer around.

Because he has a story to tell about the changes in nearly every inch of the city, some of his in-laws affectionately call him "Used To Be."

SOME THINGS ARE WORTH REMEMBERING

Rosie Phillips Dursse

There is one thing in particular that Rosie Phillips Dursse wants people to know about growing up in Charleston during the 1930s and 40s. It is that her alma mater, Memminger High School, was a very special place.

Only girls attended Memminger. The school was located at the corner of Beaufain and St. Philip Streets. "It was a beautiful grayish building," she says. "It had to be quite old." Close to the time of her graduation in 1949, city officials did an inspection of the building and found it was no longer structurally sound. So they closed it that summer and tore it down. Rivers Junior High was then converted to use as a co-ed high school, and girls were also admitted to Charleston High School from then on.

In 1954, a grammar school was built on the site of old Memminger. It was a nondescript two-story brick building that was razed in 2010 because it was found to be inadequate to withstand an earthquake, a rare but real possibility in the Lowcountry. It is being rebuilt. But the old wall still stands around the schoolyard, and the original auditorium has been renovated by the city and is used for cultural events.

"Not many people remember old Memminger High School except those of us who went there. We were the last class to graduate," Rosie explains. The next year's graduating class attended Rivers, but the graduates were allowed to receive a Memminger diploma.

"Now a lot of my former classmates meet once a month and we have lunch together. Some members of the class of 1950 meet with us. It's amazing – even after all these years, we have a lot in common and enjoy each other's company. The girls I went to school with were from all over Charleston. Some even lived in Riverland Terrace on James Island and were brought to Memminger by bus. One girl from our class became rather famous. She is a retired Saks Fifth Avenue executive and became a close friend of actress Claudette Colbert."

Rosie loves talking about her old school, but she can tell you a few other things about growing up in the city during that era. "My father had a restaurant called King Restaurant. It was at 337 King Street, in the block between Calhoun and George Streets. There were three movie houses in our same block – the Gloria, the Garden and the Majestic. The first two are still there, although they no longer function as theaters. The Majestic was between them and showed mostly cowboy movies and serials - twelve short films. Every week they'd show you one and it had a dramatic ending so you would come back each week until the series ended."

The stores on King Street had apartments above them, and many of the proprietors lived above these stores, as Rosie's family did. "It was a two-story building with a one floor apartment above the restaurant. It had large rooms and was heated with a little pot belly stove. I keep saying I'd like to go there someday and see what it's like now."

The family's surname was Filippou, "an ancient Greek name," Rosie says, and was Anglicized to Phillips. Rosie's father was a Greek immigrant, but his restaurant served Southern cuisine, since "Charlestonians had no idea what Greek cuisine was like!" Mr. Phillips had a brother who worked in the restaurant. "Uncle Johnny was a wonderful fisherman. He would go fishing and bring his catch back to the restaurant. Daddy had a large window facing the street and a large cooler looking out on King Street. They would fill the cooler with ice and large fish and other seafood that was caught that day. People would walk by and see the fresh seafood and this would bring in customers."

A lot of Greek immigrants came to Charleston in the early 20th century after Greece gained its independence from Turkey. Many had grocery stores or restaurants and lived above them. "Greeks have always been good cooks. Mother cooked Greek food upstairs for us because my father really liked it and he didn't fix it in the restaurant. So she would cook a Greek dish every day for him. We grew up eating Greek dishes."

Even though it was the Depression era, Rosie's family made a fairly good living. She says it helped that Charleston had the Navy. "Daddy would take a car and go to the Navy Yard and pass out cards. He'd tell the sailors to come to the restaurant. He'd get a lot of business that way. Even before the Second World War, he'd do this. He had a nice regular clientele, but the war is when things really started changing. There was a big difference before the war and after the war. During the war, my daddy was very busy at the restaurant. There was a lot of traffic. Before then, it was a slow way of life in Charleston."

Down King Street was another Greek family-run business - Milton Coffee House. "Everything was owned by individuals and not by chains like are there now. Many of the clothing stores were owned by Jewish families. For instance, Elza's sold clothing and Bob Ellis sold shoes. There was also LeRoy's jewelry store and Garfinkle's Jewelers. The stores on King from Calhoun to Market were more high-end. From that point on down were antique stores, like there are now. But everything was owned by local people. Every year, when the Azalea Festival was held downtown, the business owners would march down King Street in the parade. Daddy had his restaurant, so he marched in it."

Shopping for clothes was convenient for Rosie's family when they lived above the restaurant. She says, "Most of our shopping was done on King Street. The ladies dressed up to go shopping. Some would wear hats, and they wore heels and gloves. They had clips that they'd wear like a bracelet, and they'd clip their gloves on it. We really dressed up in those days."

As a child, Rosie attended Bennett School which was just around the corner from their restaurant. The school is no longer there and a college dorm now stands on the site. "We went there for four years until I was about nine. Then my father bought a house on upper St. Philip Street, where the Crosstown is now, not far from Mitchell Grammar School." Rosie and her sister attended Mitchell for two years and then went to Rivers Junior High on King Street for seventh and eighth grades. From there they went back downtown - to Memminger High School. "A lot of times we'd walk home" – a distance of about eighteen blocks (a mile and a half).

"Daddy had a car, and in the summertime he'd take us to The Battery. My mother's friends would be there also. Most of my parents' friends, especially the ladies, were Greek. The women all did embroidery and crocheting, and they'd sit and talk as we'd play on the cannons. In the winter, my daddy would take us to Hampton Park because it was too cold at The Battery. It was more comfortable there without the wind blowing. There was a zoo at Hampton Park, and we'd run around there.

"When we lived on King Street, we had a back yard behind the store, so we played there a lot. We played jump rope, ball, hopscotch, that type of thing. There was a piano store next door and my daddy would get the crates that the pianos had come in and put two together and make us a playhouse. We also used to go to The Green to play. They call it Marion Square today, but we still refer it to as 'The Green.' As kids, we could walk to the movies or to The Green. It was close to us and we were safe."

Rosie's father bought a beach house on Folly in the late 1940s. "It was on the front beach. The houses back then were strictly summer places – not the way they build them now. You couldn't spend the winter there. But we'd go every summer and spend the whole summer. The best memories I have of Folly Beach were the weekend dances at the Folly Pier. This was the 'Big Band Era' and many of the Big Bands would play there. Those were happy days with good friends. Mother sold our beach house after Daddy died in the 1950s. It was later destroyed by Hurricane Hugo."

The Phillips family attended Holy Trinity Greek Orthodox Church. The church was on St. Philip Street where the Crosstown is now. Then, land on Race Street was purchased and a new church was built there.

Rosie says, "My sister and I learned to speak Greek from our parents. It is an advantage to know a second language. My mother learned English in the restaurant. The waitresses would help her. And my father spoke English well."

Rosie remembers her father taking her with him to buy vegetables at the City Market. "He knew certain people there that he'd buy from. Everything was fresh. The buildings along Meeting Street between Market and Hasell Streets were wholesalers who sold supplies to restaurants and hotels. My sister's husband later had a restaurant across from the Charleston Hotel (on the corner of Hayne and Meeting), and they'd go to those places and buy supplies. Nobody went in that area unless they were small businessmen. It wasn't nice like it is now.

"In the 1960s, that part of the city almost closed down because everybody started moving to the suburbs. Business went down because everybody was moving out. That was a bad period. (Mayor) Joe Riley is the one that brought it back. But then all the big companies moved in downtown and there weren't local businesses anymore. Uptown has a few more individually-owned businesses. We've ridden uptown in the car and it's wonderful – they are really cleaning it up."

Rosie

Many of the buildings from Rosie's youth have not survived. Bennett School is gone. Her old church and house on St. Philip Street are both gone. Other buildings she remembers have been made into parking lots. But she says the building where her father had the restaurant is still standing. And there has always been some kind of a restaurant at 337 King Street ever since her family's restaurant was there. She says she may even eat at the current establishment someday. But she misses the fact that many of the other old buildings are now gone, in particular her high school. She wants the existence of old Memminger to have a prominent place in the history books. Rosie explains, "Memminger was just something special."

She adds, "Charleston has always had a certain charm which we just didn't realize when we were growing up."

INSIDE AND OUT

Jeanne Moseley Jeffcoat

Jeanne Moseley Jeffcoat has viewed Charleston from many different angles. Not only did she grow up in five separate neighborhoods on the peninsula, she spent time living in various suburbs, too - West of the Ashley, North Charleston, Mt. Pleasant and the Isle of Palms. And for nearly half of Mayor Joe Riley's four decades in office, she worked as his personal secretary, giving her an even more unique perspective of the city and its people.

Even when she was a child, Jeanne's life crisscrossed with some of the city's prominent and influential figures. "I was born in 1932 at Baker Hospital, and Dr. Archie Baker, one of the founders of the hospital, delivered me." She adds, "As my father was driving my mother to the hospital, he ran out of gas! So my mother had to walk the last two blocks to the hospital." As a little girl, Jeanne often went to church with her grandmother at First Baptist downtown. "I even remember attending (Reverend) Dr. John Hamrick's wedding there. I believe it was a double wedding – he and another couple both got married in the same ceremony! When I was twelve or so, I was baptized in the Rutledge Avenue Baptist Church by (Reverend) Dr. Jesse Bailey, the same minister who married Mother and Daddy."

Jeanne's family moved around the city a great deal. "I can remember living in Ashley Forest (West of the Ashley) when I was about four years old, but by the time I started school, we were back downtown, living at 19 Coming Street. My first school was Bennett School, on the corner of George and St. Philip Streets. I walked to school by myself every day, even in first grade. My mother would walk me across Wentworth Street; then I'd walk up St. Philip to George. In the afternoon, I'd walk back to the corner of Wentworth and wait for her to come and get me back across the street.

"I went to James Simons School from third to fifth grade because we had moved to the corner of King and Simons Street. It was a dirt street in those days. We lived upstairs from an ice cream store. Then, we moved to 89 Bogard Street, and I went to Mitchell School in the sixth grade and Rivers Junior High in seventh and eighth grades. For a short time, we lived in Waylyn, in the north area, and I went to Chicora for half of the ninth grade. But then we moved back into town and lived at 48 Bull Street.

"My parents owned their houses in Ashley Forest and Waylyn, but we rented when we lived in the city. I remember the house at 48 Bull as big and sitting way back off the sidewalk. There were four apartments in it. In the back was a carriage house - which is where we lived. And there were six garage apartments also. So there were a good many people living on that one lot!"

Jeanne explains, "People moved around a good bit back then. I don't know why. It really didn't bother me. We'd hate that first day at school and were a little shy at first, but we made friends. And some friends we kept. I still have friends that I met when I went to Mitchell."

Jeanne attended Memminger High School through the eleventh grade. "We moved to Mt. Pleasant, but I kept going to school at Memminger. I wasn't really supposed to go there once we moved across the Cooper, but that school year was going to be the last for Memminger, so we fudged a little bit. My grandmother lived downtown at 17 St. Philip Street, and we used her address. Daddy worked in town, so he'd bring me in to school every day and I'd ride the city bus home. I went to Moultrie my last year of high school, but I was the last 'Miss Memminger' and was crowned at Memminger Auditorium."

Jeanne says, "It was wonderful going to an all girls' school (Memminger). We had a special camaraderie, and you didn't have to compete for the boys' attention. There was a stone wall and a big iron gate – it was like a convent – and if we saw a guy peeking through the gate, we got so excited. After school, we'd just walk across the street into the back door of Woolworth's because the school was directly behind the store.

"When we were living in Mt. Pleasant, I had a Saturday job at Kress so I'd spend the night with my grandmother downtown on Friday nights. I worked from 10:00 a.m. to 7:00 p.m. on the ribbon and sewing counter. After taxes, I made $3.70 for the day. That was my spending money. And I was even able to save!"

Jeanne's first first full-time job once she was out of school was as a clerk typist at the American Tobacco Company – the Cigar Factory. "I had taken bookkeeping and business courses at Memminger. I graduated on a Friday and went right to work on Monday."

Jeanne says when she was a child, they "always did a lot of family stuff. My daddy would take my brother fishing in Colonial Lake or at The Battery, and he taught me to skate at Moultrie Playground – right where the tennis courts are now. He played on a men's softball team at Moultrie Playground. I remember going to some of his games when I was a little girl. Good memories.

"I remember going to the library on the corner of Montagu Street and Rutledge Avenue. I can't remember the name of the librarian – I want to say Miss Mamie. I used to love going there! And the old museum – it never got old for us! I was sad when it burned down, although I was surprised it didn't burn before that! It was a wonderful place – the snake room; the mummy; the stuffed polar bear.

There was a little step where you'd go up and look into a diorama. All a wonderful memory."

When they lived in the city, Jeanne says her father would sometimes take the family to Folly Beach. "He would drive straight down from the street onto the beach! We'd park in the hard sand. It was a fun place to go. But when I was teenager – once we had moved to Mt. Pleasant - I started going to the beach at the Isle of Palms and Sullivan's Island. There were also amusements at the Isle of Palms. They had a Ferris wheel and a few other rides. They got rid of them probably around the time Wild Dunes was being developed. Before then, there were just simple little houses on the island. My kids were raised on the Isle of Palms, and when they were young, there were some sand craters down by where Wild Dunes is now. The kids called it 'the moon.' I remember, one time, my daughter left me a note: 'Dear Mom – I've gone to the moon. I'll be back in time for supper.' Of course, that area has all changed."

For years, Jeanne's father worked as a type setter at Southern Printing (aka Nelson's), on the corner of Meeting and Queen Streets. "The company printed law books and school books, so he became a stickler for grammar. He was an avid reader and wrote a lot of poetry." He would often send letters and poems to the newspaper, and a number of them were printed. One of his poems lauded the completion of the old (Grace) Cooper River Bridge. It was published in the paper and later in the book, *The Great Cooper River Bridge*. There was a lot of fanfare surrounding the bridge's completion in 1929, and his poem, "An Ode to the Cooper River Bridge," describes it as 'a monster of steel' and 'a monument of which to be proud.'

Jeanne says, "Daddy always had a good job. He went to work for ten years at the *News and Courier* around the time we moved to Mt. Pleasant but went back to the printing company later. My mother told me later that the least amount of money he ever made was $15 a week – and that was during the Depression. That was pretty good money. But my mother was very careful with money. We'd eat veal cutlets two or three times a week when they were on sale. The Avenue Meat Market was on the corner of Cannon and Rutledge, but she generally just bought meat from the corner grocery. There weren't supermarkets until Rodenberg's opened uptown on Rutledge and Big Star downtown near Silver's. But every block or so had a little grocery store. Kangeter Grocery was near us when we lived on Bogard Street. When we lived at 19 Coming Street, there was a little grocery store on the next street. One time, when my brother was about five years old, he took his little wagon to that corner store and told the owner that my mother wanted a dozen of every kind of fruit he had. The store owner thought it was strange that she'd sent her little boy down there to get it, but she was a good customer and he was afraid not to give it to him. So he loaded up the wagon. Well, when my brother got it home, my mother had to walk him back to the store with all the fruit!

"Not too far from where we lived on Coming Street, there was a lady who sold eggs from her house. She kept chickens in the back yard. My mother bought from her. But my mother did all her vegetable shopping at the City Market. There were wholesale warehouses on the side, but there was nothing in the center of the Market but the fruit and vegetable vendors – in all four sheds. She'd go on Tuesdays and Saturdays because she said they were the freshest days. She'd get corn, tomatoes, butter beans, okra. We didn't eat Irish potatoes but we did get sweet potatoes. And we ate rice every day. Sometimes we'd have rice and macaroni and cheese at the same table – a lot of starches. When we had fried fish, we had cornbread."

Jeanne remembers, "There were people who would come through our neighborhood with pushcarts – kind of like a big wooden wheelbarrow – selling shrimp and crabs. I remember one of them sang, 'Shark steak - don't need noooo gravy.' Some of them would be women who would sell strawberries and black-berries. A lot of times we'd buy off the carts, particularly when we lived on Bogard Street and Rutledge. But my mother would still ride the bus downtown to the City Market twice a week and get vegetables. I'd feel sorry for those ladies when they'd see my mother coming because she was a bargainer. I remember her going to the Market right before Thanksgiving and she came home on the bus with a live turkey! And she was very thrifty. Once she bought a parakeet from Woolworth's – they sold turtles and fish and parakeets. We always had a turtle with our names on it. Anyway, the next day, the parakeet died and my mother put it back in the paper sack and took it back to Woolworth's. She made them give her another one. And they did! I guess they figured Lucy was a tough customer."

Jeanne at Hampton Park

There were certain traditions that Jeanne remembers from her youth. "Every Sunday (Easter, in particular) you went to Hampton Park. You'd go feed the ducks or have a picnic or just walk. There was a little wooden building there where they sold refreshments. And, of course, the zoo was there – a three-legged bear, a snake house, peacocks, a bird house. They had buffalo in an open space. It was just a little rinky-dink zoo but we thought it was something. Hampton Park and The Battery were always the places to go. In the spring, there was the Azalea Festival. We'd watch the parade, and then they'd have the pet parade at The Battery. People would dress up their pets and parade them on High Battery. There were mostly dogs - probably all dogs!"

At Halloween, Jeanne says, "you just rang doorbells and ran. You didn't dress up and no candy was given out. You'd just surprise somebody and hightail it out of there. And the fair would come to town every fall. It used to be held where The Citadel stadium is now. When we lived on Bogard Street, my girlfriends lived on nearby streets – Shepherd, Sumter, Fishburne – and my daddy would let me meet up with them and we'd go to the fair together. I'd start out walking by myself and hit each of their houses along the way. It would be dark - after 9 o'clock - when we'd be walking back home, and it was totally safe. I was never afraid – never had any incident that frightened me. Back then, you couldn't walk anywhere without seeing somebody you knew. Everybody knew everybody. So you didn't go on King Street unless you were dressed! You could always recognize the girls from Ashley Hall because they had on gloves."

In the summertime, Jeanne remembers, "We'd take the train to go see my maternal grandparents in Varnville in Hampton County. We'd spend the week with them. It was an 80-mile trip one way. The train station - Union Station - was on East Bay Street on the east side near Columbus Street. That area was a big hub of activity. It burned down in the late 1940s."

Jeanne says that, "On my daddy's side, several of my father's siblings lived for a brief time in the Charleston Orphan House on Calhoun Street. When my grandfather died, she put four of them in there until she could make some money to take care of them. My aunt was just an infant. But that happened in a lot of families. In fact, many of the kids who went to Bennett School with me lived at the old orphan house.

"After my grandfather died, my grandmother ran a boarding house on Spring Street where a lot of the workers who were building the Ashley River Bridge stayed. She ended up remarrying - a doctor from McClellanville. They met one day at the Woolworth's store on King Street. He was a sweet old gentleman who owned the only drugstore in McClellanville. His drugstore is now used by the historical society out there."

Jeanne recalls a few big events in Charleston. "When WCSC was just a radio station, they'd broadcast from the top floor of the Francis Marion Hotel. When I was six or eight, they had the 'Stars of Tomorrow' every Saturday morning. Local people would come on the show and sing. I don't remember what I sang, but I sang on the radio! The emcee was Russell Long – Uncle Russ, they called him. It was thrilling for us.

"We were one of the first families in Mt. Pleasant to have a television. When the huge antenna was being put on our roof, there must've been two hundred people watching. They must've thought, 'The Moseleys are rich – they are getting a TV!' But Charleston didn't even have a TV station yet! The closest TV station was WBTE in Charlotte. Occasionally, we might see snow with a figure on it on our TV. WCSC was the first TV station here – that was an exciting time. I remember Charlie Hall saying, 'Channel 5 is now alive!' I don't even remember when the other stations came along."

Another exciting event was when "President Franklin Roosevelt came through the city one time. I have a vague memory of going to Union Station and seeing him on the back of the train. I also remember there were a lot of service people here in the 1940s. My brother and I would stand on the corner of King and Simons Streets, and truck after truck with servicemen would go by. We'd wave to them. They were probably being put on or off a ship. Market Street was filled with sailors during that time."

But a few of the events Jeanne remembers aren't such fond memories. "I remember in the late '30s – I was in first or second grade - there was a tornado that tore up the Market. I also remember a hurricane when we were living in Mt. Pleasant. That must've been the early '50s. My daddy was working at night at the newspaper, and his car was one of the last to come across the bridge before they closed it. He said how the bridge was really shaking!"

Jeanne continues, "But I can't remember being scared about the storms back then. People didn't leave. I think the storms are more fierce now. When Hugo hit in 1989, my husband and I were living on the Isle of Palms. We had four feet or more of the ocean in the house - and we were three blocks away from the beach! Mayor Riley was extremely visionary about Hugo. I was working in his office at the time, and he said to me, 'Jeanne, we're going to have more water in this city than we've ever seen before.' We stayed at my daughter's house in Summerville with my mother and daddy. We didn't know if we still had a home for at least a week because the bridge to Sullivan's Island was out and there was no other bridge to the island back then. George Campsen, who owned the tour boat to Fort Sumter, gave island residents a ride to the marina on the Isle of Palms, and we had three hours to go and check on our house. We had to walk twenty blocks from the marina to our house. We held hands as we approached the house and saw the big tree in the front yard. We were glad it was still there. But we had a boat on a trailer – someone else's - in our front yard. There was a headboard from someone's bed. And, oh, the smell - this was a week after the storm! Some people might have stayed after that day, but there was no electricity or plumbing - and no way to get food - so we hurried to get back to 41st Street to catch the boat. I understand there was a 16 foot wall of water that washed over the island. The eye entered Breach Inlet, but if it had entered on Edisto Island, Charleston would've been destroyed.

"Working in the mayor's office during that post-Hugo period was tough. But people were wonderful. From all over the country, we got offers of help. I think the thing I remember the most was a letter Mayor Riley got from a couple in North Charleston. If you recall, President George H.W. Bush came to North Charleston and met with its mayor, John Bourne. The president didn't come into Charleston. I know North Charleston had its share of damage, but this couple wrote to Mayor Riley and said they appreciated all he had done for the people in and around the Charleston area. I remember their words very distinctly. They wrote, 'President Bush may have had his arms around Mayor Bourne, but you, sir, had your arms around the people.' It brought tears to my eyes. But he did - and he even had losses himself. It was a sad time – but a rewarding time, too. I don't know when the man slept. Nobody worked harder than Joe Riley. I don't know that we would've recovered as quickly or as completely without his leadership. He was a strong hand and, as far as I'm concerned, he is ten feet tall. He adores his city and adores the people in it. His biggest fault is that he works too damn hard. It's not a 9-to-5 job. But Joe Riley doesn't ask any more of anybody than he does of himself. And he'll thank you and praise you for the work you do. It makes you want to work even harder. Everybody who knows him respects him."

There were a number of memorable occasions Jeanne had while working in the mayor's office. "I have a picture of Prince Charles holding my hand. The police photographer took a picture at that very moment. Not everybody gets to shake the hand of the future King of England! He truly was a 'Prince Charming.' You were the only one in the world when he spoke to you – he looked directly into your eyes. I also met the Duke and Duchess of Hapsburg. I met some interesting local people in Mayor Riley's office, too. I remember one little old lady came in without an appointment. I asked, 'Can I help you?' She insisted no, that it was 'between me, Jesus and Mayor Riley.' I told her the mayor wasn't available so she said she'd come back. She never did, but when I told the mayor about her later, he said, 'At least she put me in good company.'"

Jeanne started working in City Hall in 1976 as an assistant to Jay Shine, the first African-American attorney for the city. (He was also the first black graduate of The Citadel.) She went to work in the mayor's office the following year and retired from there in 1995. At that time, Joe Riley and Jeanne had both worked in City Hall about the same number of years.

Jeanne was born at a time when many Charlestonians were 'too poor to paint and too proud to whitewash.' She now sees a Charleston that is a glittering gem of a city. Not only has she witnessed this jewel's extraction, she was right there with the visionaries who helped polish it.

You could say that she knows Charleston inside and out.

THAT RINGS A BELL

Creighton Hay

Creighton Hay's boyhood home was at 160 Calhoun Street. At the time, dozens of other boys and girls also called that address their home. They lived at the Charleston Orphan House.

"We were referred to as 'the children from 160 Calhoun Street.' They didn't call us orphans. In fact, I don't know anyone there who was a true orphan. We all had parents who were alive.

"Those were tough times. In fact, my high school English teacher, who was from a well-known, old Charleston family, said that even many of the South of Broad people didn't have money and had to take in boarders. During the Second World War, the orphan house was loaded with people dropping their kids off. Most didn't stay as long as I did. I was five when I went in, my kid brother was three, and my older brother was ten. My family had lived on Poinsett Street, but when my father died in 1938, my mother put the three of us in the orphan house the next year. I stayed until it closed in 1951. My older brother stayed until he joined the service. They would help you to leave when you turned eighteen.

"You'd be surprised at the people around here who lived at the orphan house. One girl became a Republican representative in the state house. A guy became a doctor. Another became a supervisor at either Ford or GM. And one became a lawyer and married the daughter of a U.S. Senator. When I was teaching at Trident Tech in the 1960s, a man there stopped me in the hall and said, 'Didn't you live at 160 Calhoun Street?' He had been there, too. And the superintendant when I was at the orphan house – Miss Dora Schwettmann - had grown up in the orphanage herself. She spent her whole life there. She went to work in the sewing room as a young woman and worked her way up. The orphan house had been around a long time even before I lived there. Andrew Buist Murray lived there – he is the one Murray Boulevard and Murray School are named after. And so did Christopher Memminger," a member of the Confederate Cabinet.

Creighton has a book about the orphan house that was put together by a man who had lived there as a child. He turns to a picture of a young girl on one of its pages. "She grew up there and they finally forced her out at 21. She was there longer than anyone. She became a hairdresser and would go back and fix their hair." Another photo shows a young woman who was not a resident there but Creighton explains, "She started a phys ed program for us while she was going to Winthrop. She later became a lawyer and was on city council."

The orphan house was a huge building. The property took up two-thirds of the block of Calhoun Street between King and St. Philip Streets. "There were two fields in the back near Vanderhorst Street where we played baseball and football. There were two other fields in the front facing Calhoun Street. One field was for girls to play and the other was for boys. We couldn't intermingle - but some-times we'd find a way! Eventually, around 1949, they let the boys go on the girls' side and the next year, they let the girls' go over to boys' side.

"We had baseball teams that played in a league against the city parks' teams – Hampton Park, Moultrie Playground. We coached ourselves – and got in a lot of fights. But we had good fun. I played different positions. I was a left-handed catcher and left-handed first baseman - with a right-handed glove! We made do with what we had. For football, there were different teams based on age and weight limits – the fleas, mites and midgets. I played on all three because I was small and they never knew how old I was."

Creighton says that Mr. Ohlandt, who was a food distributor for the grocery business, was chairman of the board of the directors at the orphan house. "He used to send us a big truck of watermelons every summer and we'd just gorge ourselves! Mr. Ohlandt had a big four-door sedan and he had a chauffeur. One day, we were walking home to the orphan house after a game, and he stopped and piled us all in the big old car and drove us home. We were riding in style!"

The orphan house had its own Boy Scout troop - #22 – sponsored by Citadel Square Baptist Church. "We used to go to Camp Ho Nan Wah out on Wadmalaw Island every year. And we had our own kindergarten – in fact it was the first kindergarten in the state. They'd also had a school there years before, but when I was there, we went to Bennett Grammar School, then to Rivers Junior High and Charleston High or Murray Vocational."

There was a chapel in the back of the property, facing Vanderhorst Street. "It was old-looking on the outside but was beautiful inside. There was a Tiffany window and two beautiful paintings. One of the paintings is now hanging in St. Luke's Chapel at the Medical University. I was surprised to see it when I went to a wedding there awhile back." The other painting which depicts Christ blessing the children now hangs in Cherokee Place Methodist Church in North Charleston.

"We were all Protestants kids – the Catholics had their own orphanage," Creighton says. "Our matrons were big church-goers and one had been a missionary in China. We had ministers come to our chapel on Sunday afternoons. There was one old man who was on stand-by. He ran the Star Gospel Mission which took care of the poor people above Line Street. He was a riot and loved coming to preach to us on Sunday afternoons. We had our own Sunday school in the morning which we took care of ourselves. After Sunday school, you could go to outside churches if you wanted. We were steered by the matrons to Citadel Square Baptist Church, so some kids went there. One of the boys in my age group ended up later becoming the pastor there – Donald Berry. I was baptized there at the age of 12. Sometimes I'd go by myself, but other times I'd tell them I was going to church but I'd go straight down King Street to the Battery. I'd just sit there and look out at the water and boats. I liked walking and loved sitting there. Still do. And I loved passing by the old buildings."

Creighton says, "On Saturday, you could go see your parents. Sometimes, I'd ride the bus to see my mother in North Charleston. She was in bad health and didn't come to see us much. As I got older, I visited her less and less but still kept in touch with her, even when I was in the military."

In August 1951, the orphanage closed and the children were moved to a new location named Oak Grove on Lackawanna Boulevard in North Charleston, near Park Circle. In the late 1970s, the name was changed again to Carolina Youth Development Center. Creighton shows another picture from the book. "This is the statue that stood on top of the cupola of the old orphan house. They found it in a ditch at the new place. How in the hell it got there and how anybody allowed that to happen is sacrilege!" The statue is now on display at the Charleston Museum.

Another photo in the book was taken the day the kids were moving to the new place. "Notice how these kids are dressed - in nice new clothes." Then he pulls out a photo that's not in the book. It was taken back in his day. It shows about a dozen boys, all around the age of ten, in worn, patched clothes – obviously hand-me-downs. Many are wearing pants that are too short for them. Creighton says it was taken in 1943. "Notice the difference? The one in the book was taken by the newspaper. The kids are almost posed. This other one is candid. Notice the guy holding up a bicycle tire around his face. We played with anything!"

Creighton thinks he's in the picture but he's not sure. And one of the boys in the photo didn't live at the orphan house. "His grandmother worked there, so he'd come and play. Two of these boys were in the Army in Korea when I was there. We didn't know it at the time but found out later that we'd been stationed about twenty miles from each other! Once, I was in a jeep and was stopped at a checkpoint by an MP who had also been in the orphan house at the same time I was! We couldn't believe it! So four of us were all within a twenty-mile radius in Korea at the same time!"

Creighton flips to another page in the book and shows a photo of girls wearing uniforms with pinafores. The picture was taken at a picnic at Otranto in Goose Creek. "Every May, they took us out there on the train. They also took us to the circus downtown every year. And they took us to the beach – Folly Beach. They'd put us on buses and take us out there. We'd go out there a lot."

The orphan house had an indoor swimming pool that was fed by an artesian well. "We went swimming in there pretty regularly in the summer. Before you got in the pool, you had to take a bath or shower. There was a man there who would check to make sure you were clean. And if you weren't, he'd swat you with a belt. We wondered why he didn't swat the older boys who were supposed to be making sure we were clean!"

The younger boys were wards of the older boys. Creighton explains, "When I was older, I had fifteen kids under my care, including my younger brother. It was my job to make sure they took a bath and to get them up each morning and make sure they washed their face, brushed their teeth. We also made their beds – or stripped the beds if they had wet them. The matrons were elderly so we had to do it."

Another photo in the book shows the children eating in the dining hall. "It was a big room with a lot of different tables. We were adequately fed - none of the meals were big but they were nutritious. There weren't many fat boys, but we didn't starve either. We ate a lot of green beans and tomato soup - which I will not eat to this day. Supper wasn't much. Maybe some peaches and a slice of bread and peanut butter - and we didn't eat again for twelve hours. We had black cooks, and if you became friendly with them, they'd give you a little extra. One really liked me. They cooked in big copper pots and also made brown bag lunches for us to take to school."

The kids slept in large dormitory-style rooms filled with single beds – similar to old hospital beds. Children were grouped according to age. But when Creighton was sixteen, he and two other boys shared a small room on the top floor. "We could see the clock on St. Matthew's Church and we used it to tell time. We could also see the Francis Marion Hotel. One time when the American Legion was staying there, I twisted a towel around my upper waist like a bra, and from that distance, they couldn't tell that I was not a girl. I didn't mind doing crazy things like that."

On the top floor of the orphan house – the fifth floor – there was a sick ward which was called 'the hospital.' Creighton says, "They could even do minor operations like tonsillectomies. Two ladies stayed there. They were sisters and they helped in various capacities at the orphanage. I'll tell you a funny story. When I was with the Boy Scouts, we went for a couple days to Bull's Island. We went swimming in the water - with no clothes on, of course. Later, we were walking on the path and I stepped off the path to relieve myself. Unbeknownst to me, there was poison oak! I swelled up and had to go into our hospital and lay in bed with a hunk of gauze with witch hazel on it. Some of the girls came up and wanted to see it, so I showed it to them. I was proud of it! I was about twelve years old."

At the orphan house, there were two indoor playrooms for boys and girls to use on bad-weather days. "There were no toys or anything in there. We'd just run around in there and play. But most of the time, we got out in the yard and played. You were on your own after you got up in the morning because you couldn't go back to your room. But we couldn't leave the campus, as we called it, without permission. I came and went as I pleased because I could always climb the fence! And I also had the keys because one of my jobs was to lock the gates at night. Another job I had was to get the paper in the morning through a hole in the wall. We called the wall our 'begging wall.' As people came by, we'd say, 'Please, suh, a nickel to buy a baseball bat.' But we'd use it to buy candy. When I was older, the matrons would give us money to ride the bus to junior high school. I'd keep the money and meet my friend around the corner at a mom and pop store, and he'd ride me to school on his bicycle."

Creighton explains that the children had individual boxes or cubbies in which to keep their personal belongings. "Or we'd put them under the mattress so nobody would take them. We had as good a Christmas as anybody. You'd get whatever your parents could give you, but also the Kiwanis Club would give us a party, and three other social clubs gave us presents. We got great

Creighton in the play yard at 160 Calhoun Street

presents. And Joan Simmons School of Dance – which was the only one around at the time – would bring her troupe to the orphan house and perform for us. During the Second World War, we got skates from the people at the Navy Yard when you couldn't buy them. And we'd put on a Christmas program for the community in the chapel. We'd sing about fifteen to twenty songs. We must've done an excellent job because the chapel was always packed with visitors. We had a *monster* organ in that chapel, and a renowned organist from the community played at the performance."

Creighton admits, "You could always tell us from the Catholic Orphan House boys. They were well-behaved and we were raucous. I'm sure people made comments. But we weren't really bad. Both orphanages would be together at the parties at the Navy Yard. We also had one at the ballroom at the Francis Marion Hotel. You could look at a picture and pick out the Charleston Orphan House kids.

"The older kids had a few chores – and the younger ones took on chores as they grew. When I was young, my job was to put the bread out on the tables before a meal and put it back in the bread room after the meal, if there was any left. The girls cleaned up the tables. We had a laundry room and did our own laundry. That's where I learned to iron shirts. Also, the boys had to go out in the yard and hang the big blankets after they were washed. There were big wringers we had to put them through first.

"The girls learned to sew but the boys weren't taught any skills. All I ever learned to do was shovel coal. We had to go to the coal shed and put the coal in a wheelbarrow and roll it to the main building to be used in the coal-fired boiler which produced steam for cooking and heating. I was not even a hundred pounds and was doing that! It was hard work. But there were not really too many chores."

Because Creighton was older than most of the kids at the orphan house, his friends were mainly from school. "Everyone knew each other and we went out together in large groups. I had one good friend and I'd spend weekends with him or sometimes go to his house to eat. I had another good friend from an old Charleston family and his mother would call the orphan house and ask if I could walk home and play with him."

Creighton had a number of recreational activities away from the orphanage. "I played football for St. Patrick's Church, and we had games on the Green (Marion Square) every Saturday morning. I could go to the movies by myself, even when I was young. Once they sent my older brother to look for me because I didn't come home on time. I had gone to three movies. He finally found me. I don't know where I got the money."

Creighton says that everything was within walking distance of the orphan house. "You couldn't ask for a better location. We had an expense account at the barber shop next to the Garden Theater, just below Calhoun. We used to go in the little shops on King Street. The matrons would call you in and they'd send you to get something at one of the stores if you needed it. We had an expense account for shoes at Levy's on the corner of Liberty and King Streets. You had your good pair of shoes which were kept in a shoe box in the shoe room at the orphan house. You'd go get them on Sunday morning and wear them to church and return them to the shoe room in the afternoon.

"Our shoe room was on the second floor near where the super-intendent's bedroom was. If you got in trouble, you had to sit on the stairs outside her room and she'd keep an eye on you. I sat on those stairs many times, usually for taking off. I was independent and into mischief. One time when I was a teenager, one of the matrons told me to do something and I told her no. She kept up and finally I told her to 'go blow.' I ended up sitting on the steps for that!

"Occasionally, we had matron's night out. She didn't really go out – she just kept her door closed. So then, the older boys had to watch the younger ones – they'd babysit. They had a 'mental notebook' where they would list all the things we 'supposedly' did wrong – and then they'd whack you with a broom. Sometimes they'd whack you on the hands and you didn't even know what you did wrong. Years later, some of those older boys would come back to visit and I thought how I hated those boys. But I don't regret those days – it could've been worse."

Like boys often do, kids in the orphan house fought with each other, but there were no gangs – no cliques. "And at school, you did not fool with orphan house boys because there was so many of us. When it was cold or raining, we all wore black coats - like capes – and descended on that school (Bennett)!"

Creighton says, "As a teenager, I went to the beach with friends. We very seldom went in the water. It was just a good party time at the beach in those days. When I was about fifteen or so, we'd also go to pool parlors. There was one called the M&M on the corner of King Street and Burns Lane. We spent a lot of time at the M&M. They had magazines there and we'd read comic books and play pool. I have a picture of some of the people there, most of whom were friends of mine, and the joke was we all had cigarettes dangling from our mouths but none of us smoked! The man who ran it was rumored to be the stepfather of the actress Lauren Bacall. Another man who ran it married a woman whose siblings were once in the orphan house."

From his days at the orphan house, there were a couple of particular events that stick out in Creighton's mind. "I remember an ice storm one year. One of the guys from the orphan house was running across Calhoun Street to catch the bus and slipped and slid under the bus. He went in one side and out the other - and was not hurt!" Before his time, Creighton had an older brother at the orphan house who fell off the monkey bars and contracted blood poising from a compound fracture. He died in the old Roper hospital. Creighton adds, "My stepfather had a son who was in the orphan house and was run over by a truck when they had everybody out there to the beach. He also died."

Another event Creighton remembers from his boyhood was when he was eight years old. "It was December 7, 1941. We heard the newsboys down on Calhoun Street calling out, 'Extra, Extra.' All we knew was that war was bad, but we didn't know how it affected us. Several boys who grew up in the orphan house before me died in the Second World War. Another boy from when I was there was killed on the second day of the Korean War. He had won the state championship for marble shooting when he was a kid at the orphan house."

When Creighton was twelve, the Kiwanis Club had a program in which their members would 'adopt' a boy who was interested in the field they worked in. "One boy wanted to be a doctor, another wanted to be an engineer. I wanted to be a pilot," he explains. "There was a man who had a private plane and he took me flying. Then he took me out to lunch at the old Squirrel Inn in Summerville. It was where rich people used to go in the summertime. We went on a Sunday for dinner. It was hard for me to maneuver in that well-mannered crowd! I remember they had a big dog – a Saint Bernard - walking around through the restaurant. It was a beautiful dog – I'll never forget that."

Everybody at the orphan house had a nickname. "They called me Skinny – and I was! My brother was Six Toes for obvious reasons, and my younger brother was Goat because he chewed paper when he was very young. My older brother was called Droopy Drawers, later shortened to Droopy, presumably because his clothes never fit him."

Creighton says, "This was what life was. I didn't know anything else. I don't remember anything about life before then and I don't remember my father at all. But I have a torn picture of him. He was an ambulance driver in World War I."

The orphan house was run with city funds and private donations. Creighton explains, "I could've gone to medical college and had it paid for by the orphan house funds, but I looked at eight to ten years of school and didn't want to go that long. I really wanted to be a psychologist, but engineers made more money. And the two guys I'd roomed with at the orphan house went to the University of South Carolina and studied engineering, so I did the same thing. The orphan house paid for the first two years of college; then you had to pay for yourself."

Creighton says he always enjoyed school. "I had great teachers at Charleston High. Mr. Griffin, Mr. Seabrook, and Mr. Gibbs. I enjoyed high school – I really did. I only cut one day. We just left and went to Murray School for some reason and then rode around. Mr. Griffin looked out for me – got me a little job working at a shoe store – and in my senior year he had me elected chairman of the senior board while the kids at the orphan house were quarantined for the first two weeks of the school year because of a polio scare. He also selected me to attend Boys State as one of two representatives from Charleston High in 1950. It was prestigious and was held at a school in Columbia. He was great! I remember when the Carolina-Clemson game was played in 1949, he brought a radio to class and let the students listen to it. One of the questions on his exam was, 'Who ran the first touchdown around the world?' It was Magellan.

"And I can remember every teacher I had in elementary school. My fourth and fifth-grade teacher got us on the radio show at WCSC on top of the Francis Marion Hotel. And my sixth-grade history teacher - I always had an interest in history and really picked up an affinity for it.

"I took a lot of things from the orphan house also, but two that really stuck are a love for classical music – opera – and a love of reading. We had our own library there – a well-stocked library.

I read all the Tarzan books, cowboy books, National Geographic. After I did my homework in our study hall – and we had to show it - I could go upstairs to the library. I love it to this day and read all the time. We got a well-rounded education for life. At the orphan house, one of the matrons would leave her door open at night and she'd play her radio. So on Monday nights, we'd listen to Firestone Presents and Bell Telephone Hour. We'd listen to all the classical music while we were going to sleep."

Creighton says, "I never regretted growing up in the orphan house. I didn't know anything different. All my friends in high school knew but nobody ever pointed it out.

"I wasn't in Charleston when they took it down. I was in the Army and didn't keep in contact with anybody, so I didn't know. But I would've been upset if I knew they were taking the whole building down. That was a big part of my life."

Creighton became the second alumnus of the orphan house to serve as its chairman of the board. Andrew Buist Murray was the first. "Starting in 1975, we had a reunion every year of all the kids from the orphan house. You'd be surprised at the alumni around here. But we've started dying off. "

There is a painting of the Charleston Orphan House which hung for years on the wall of the College of Charleston's dorm at the site of the original orphan house. The painting is now hanging at the Carolina Youth Development Center. It was painted by an alumnus of the orphan house. And there is a historical plaque on the wall of the College's bookstore which is also on the original site. There are plaques at the current North Charleston location of the orphan house, too. But there is a large bell there that may better tell the story of the scores of children whose formative years were spent at 160 Calhoun Street. Creighton says, "That bell hung in the cupola of the old orphan house. One time, a couple of us crept up into the attic and carved our initials in the bell. The bell fell when they tore down the old building." But the bell is still solid.

Creighton adds, "The bell sat in a prominent location at the North Charleston location, in front of the admin building facing Lackawanna Boulevard, but was moved several years ago to a very elegant garden setting at another location on the campus. I attended the dedication ceremony and felt at last I had come back to my childhood home."

A DIFFERENT SLANT ON
CHARLESTON

J. Martin Moseley

Marty Moseley grew up on Radcliffe Street in the 1930s and 40s. "My house was around the corner from St. Patrick's Catholic Church. It was also three blocks - and a million miles - from Ashley Hall School. White Anglo-Saxon Protestants were a distinct minority where we lived. Our neighborhood was mixed ethnically and racially. There was a large number of black children. The white kids were Irish and Lebanese Catholics and Jews."

When Marty grew up, most people in Charleston rented their homes, and like many other families, Marty's moved around a good bit within the same neighborhood. Often, people living under one roof consisted of aunts, uncles, cousins, grandparents – and sometimes even friends. For instance, Marty's cousin lived on Maple Street in a house full of people – all relatives. As an adult, Marty once asked him where everybody slept. The answer was probably quite common: They all just shared bedrooms. Nobody really had their own bed and they went to sleep in whatever bed was available at the time.

Also typical, Marty says, was the fact that "the church was a very important part of your recreational life, especially if you were Catholic. Every parish had a parochial school, and we spent a lot of time in the afternoons in the school yard as well as in the church yard. I was an altar boy. During Lent, I served Mass every morning – early, when the chickens were crowing in nearby yards. One day after school, my next-door neighbor and I decided to cut altar boy practice and go to a Laurel and Hardy movie at the American Theater. We could've gone around the block to get there and avoided passing too close to the church, but there was no sport in that. So we decided to run the gauntlet! We heard Father Patat shout, 'There they are!' All the boys gave chase and brought us back to practice.

"Many of us belonged to the Boy Scouts which, to my memory, was always organized around a church. My troop was #13, one of the city's largest, and was at St. Patrick's Church. Other large troops were at Holy Communion Episcopal Church on Ashley Avenue, St. Matthew's Lutheran on King, and the Jewish Community Center on St. Philip Street.

"Much of the lives of children (especially boys) revolved around the city playgrounds. There were about ten on the peninsula and these were often defined by the different neighborhoods. There were regular season games of competitive sports - football, base-ball - and the scores were published in the newspaper. Umpires and refs were usually older boys. The thought of a parent getting involved was never conceived and I can't ever recall seeing a par-ent at a game. No one had a uniform or equipment except for their own baseball glove. The playground did, however, furnish a catcher's mask.

"On summer nights, we played I Spy, Kick the Can, Cops and Robbers, and Half Rubber in the streets until our mothers called us in. We didn't leave the neighborhood much except to go to another playground to play ball. I delivered the *Evening Post* for a while but mostly we just played a lot. I got my first real job at age 14 as a soda jerk at Schwettmann's Pharmacy. It was, all in all, a pretty idyllic storybook existence.

"As we got to be in our teens, however, we learned there was more going on in Charleston than church and playgrounds and playing ball in the street. What we learned delighted us - Charleston almost entirely ignored the state's stringent liquor laws! No one ever had a problem getting a drink in Charleston - at any time. Liquor sold by the drink in saloons or in restaurants was illegal and no beer was to be sold on Sundays, but in Charleston, those laws were totally ignored. In restaurants, alcohol was even on the menu! Minors had little difficulty being served in saloons which were all over the city. Market Street was one sleazy saloon after another. Drinks were hustled by women known as 'B' girls – 'Buy me a drink, honey?' – who tacitly promised more than alcohol, a promise which I believe was seldom fulfilled. It would be a rare boy who grew up in Charleston who didn't have some story regarding Market Street or some other area like it.

"There was also open prostitution in Charleston but it was confined to red light districts. The most prominent of these was the area around Archdale and West Streets. West Street was notorious, and every house on the street was a brothel. Prostitution was wide open. The ladies' names were well-known and were even listed in the telephone book!

"Gambling was also open in bars and in some pool rooms. The biggest pool room I remember was the M&M, but it was not just some den of iniquity. Some customers were in there to shoot pool, but more than occasionally, poker and blackjack were played on the tables. There were also direct wires to get the scores for big-time sporting events. Scores were posted on a blackboard, and there was a big counter for placing bets on the events. There were tables for a variety of games and big chairs around the room where you could sit and watch the pool games. It was particularly interesting when two sharks were playing for money or when a hustler was taking advantage of someone who thought he could shoot pool. Of course, there were slot machines which were in many bars and also in most private clubs and fraternal organization halls.

"Such practices were wide open and had been for generations, but of course it couldn't happen without the complicity of the city administration and police – not to mention the consent and agreement of the population. Charleston was an urban oasis in a rural state. It had a diverse population and an old-world tolerance of what the rest of the state considered sin. Few Charlestonians wanted outsiders (state government) tampering with the social life of the city. The occasional vice raids from the state – which most often came with plenty of warning from local officials – brought great indignation on the part of the city's population, from the South of Broad elite to the ethnically-mixed populations of the boroughs and Little Mexico to the middle class neighborhoods of the north and northwest of the city. However, the raids (which were never imposed on brothels) and the ensuing fines were simply the cost the city charged for doing business. Charleston was this way for at least the first half of the 20th century.

"Politics was also a great sport in the city, and going to a rally at one of the playgrounds or at College Park was a delight. In my youth and certainly before, there was only one political party in the state – the Democratic Party. It was the party of segregation and white supremacy. Blacks were disenfranchised. The GOP was considered the party of Lincoln and Reconstruction, and there were virtually no Republicans around. Every single office holder in the state was a Democrat. The Democratic primary was tantamount to election, since there was no real competition from Republicans in the general election.

"But there were factions within the Democratic Party which, for decades, were largely defined by the rivalry dating to the mayoral campaign between John P. Grace and Thomas Stoney around the time of the First World War. Grace was an Irish-Catholic politician from the Borough (Ansonborough) and the first to buck the old Charleston establishment. His rival, Stoney, was a street-wise tough cookie like Grace and lived uptown but was a member of the downtown establishment. He attended St. Michael's Church and was a member of the St. Cecilia Society, the Elks Club and the Knights of Pythias. For the next twenty-five years, the politics of Charleston was personified as Grace versus the Charleston elite, the progressive movement versus the old establishment. The campaigns were bitter, and there were disappearing ballot boxes - and even murder.

"Incidents involving issues of race, police fraud, and violence were routine. Religion and ethnicity was very often a factor. Grace's supporters were from the East Side, the Borough and the neighborhood surrounding St. Patrick's Church. He also had a lot of German support due to his opposition to the First World War. The campaign of 1919 was vicious, religiously-charged, and marked by much fraud and violence.

"These two factions lasted until my day. In 1951, the mayoral campaign was between O.T. Wallace and William M. Morrison. Wallace had inherited the Grace mantle, and Morrison's campaign manager was none other than Thomas Stoney. Grace was dead, but Stoney, although quite old, was very much alive. Morrison was the victor.

"By the next election, things had changed in the game of politics – blacks could vote and there was television. The press was becoming very inquisitive and federal courts also were becoming very interested here. The campaign of 1959 was on TV. Morrison was running for re-election against the young, good-looking, and squeaky clean Palmer Gaillard."

Gaillard's victory began his sixteen-year term and signaled the beginning of a new era for Charleston, one that would usher in huge changes - and a new identity - for the city.

Note: The quotes above were taken from lecture notes of the late J. Martin Moseley who died in 2012.

HARBORING MEMORIES

Arthur Joye (Skipper) Jenkins, Jr.

Not many people can say that they lived on the campus of both the Old Citadel and the 'new' Citadel. Nor can they say they spent their childhood at the school. But Skipper Jenkins can. That's because his stepfather was a Citadel professor and his family lived in the teachers' housing. "We had a grand time. All the professors' children were about my age. We went to the canteen and the swimming pool on campus and played on the tennis courts when the cadets weren't using them. I can remember asking Mama, 'Why don't we join the yacht club or the country club?' and she said, 'You've got a country club right up here at The Citadel.'"

Skipper's family has deep roots in Charleston. "My father, Arthur Joye Jenkins, Sr., was born on Edisto Island. My mother, Elise Cart, was born downtown at 14 Gadsden Street. From what Mama has told me, we were living on Montagu Street when I was born. My father died in an automobile accident when I was ten months old, so my mother, older sister and I moved in with my grandmother at 14 Gadsden. We lived with her there for two or three years. Then Mama met my stepfather playing Bridge. He was a chemistry professor at The Citadel and later became head of the department. Eventually, he became dean. The new chemistry building, Byrd Hall, is named for him.

"When they were first married, we lived at the Old Citadel." The school had moved to its current site the decade before, but the housing for the professors was still at the old campus at Marion Square, on the King Street side. "They were building about thirty new houses and apartments at the new campus and hadn't finished them yet. When they did, we moved over there. I was about five. Then they tore down the ones at the old place and built the county library on King Street. The part that's now the Embassy Suites Hotel on Meeting Street was originally classrooms and the barracks. And it wasn't painted pink the way it is now."

Although Skipper never knew his biological father, he was very close with his Jenkins relatives. "I spent a lot of time on Edisto with my aunts. We moved out there for the summer during the polio scare in 1939. All the Jenkins cousins who lived in the city went out there. And during World War II, I had an aunt who would say, 'We want you to come out and stay - but we want you to bring sugar because we don't have any!'

"One of my aunts and I used to go shrimping out there. She was my favorite aunt. We'd ride downriver on the ebb and when the tide changed, we'd come back with it. We made hand lines – fishing lines – together. Those old gals grew up down there with very little money after the Civil War. Their brother – my uncle - was Micah Jenkins. People used to call him 'Mr. Republican' when the Republican Party first began growing big in South Carolina."

Another of Skipper's aunts was Elizabeth Jenkins Young whom Mayor Joe Riley once described as 'the embodiment of preservation in Charleston.' "She was my father's half-sister. My grandmother died from cancer when my daddy was four, and my grandfather remarried. He had three children from his second marriage and five from his first marriage. My daddy was the youngest from the first and Aunt Liz was from the second. They all grew up out there on Edisto at Brick House Plantation. In 1929, the big house burned to the ground. The ruins are still there and we all have smaller houses built around it." Skipper has a framed photograph of the big house, the home of Edward Jenkins, his grandfather. "The house was built in 1725 by Paul Hamilton. They say that in the basement – the ground level – there were vents that faced outward to keep Indians from climbing in."

On the other side of his family, Skipper's maternal grandfather owned a jewelry store on King Street. "W.P. Cart Jewelers was three or four doors above the Riviera Theater. His store was there during my entire childhood and was still there when we got married. Naturally, I bought my wife's ring from the store. The house that my mother grew up in (#14 Gadsden Street) is still there but the family no longer owns it. It was given to my mother's father by his father. I used to love to stay there with my grandmother when I was growing up. We'd go to church on Sunday at Grace Episcopal and then I'd stay with my grandparents and go to a movie. A lot of times we'd do that; we had fun. I remember one time when I was about six years old, my sister and I were there while my parents were on a trip. A hurricane came through and the area flooded. We dove off the front steps into the water and swam around to the back! Hurricanes went through two or three times when I was young. We didn't run; nobody ran."

Skipper's mother was one of six children so he had a lot of family on her side, too. But they lived downtown and Skipper lived uptown. He attended James Simons Grammar School and Rivers High School. Skipper says, "By the time I was in high school, they had closed Memminger girls' school, and we got a lot of old maid teachers – tough ones - from Memminger. That was probably the only reason I got out of it!"

When Skipper was growing up, most of his friends lived at The Citadel. "We always had a bunch of us from The Citadel walking to school together. And we didn't play much at The Battery or Hampton Park; we mainly played at The Citadel. As soon as school was out for the summertime, the shoes came off and we were running around barefooted and sunburned. The cadets were gone for the summer and we had the whole campus to ourselves. When

I was fourteen or so, our group of Citadel kids used to pack a little lunch and ride our bicycles all the way to Angel Oak. There wasn't much traffic on Maybank Highway and there were a bunch of us. It was an adventure! There was no fence or anything in those days. You'd just go walk around on the limbs and carve your name on it. We didn't know who owned it and didn't care. Everything was fine, and we'd be gone the whole day."

Much of Skipper's summer was also spent on Edisto with his father's family. "But I do remember going to Folly Beach sometime. I remember there were a couple of rides on Folly and they had slot machines in the pavilion out there. Slot machines were really all over the place. Even when I was grown and became a member of the Carolina Yacht Club, they still had them. One lady used to come in there every day and spend $100 a day on the slot machine. But the county got very serious about gambling in the late '60s and early '70s. They had to clamp down and take them out. We were sorry to lose them because having those slot machines used to keep the dues down. We always thought the rest of the state didn't like Charleston because we would do anything we wanted to do when we wanted to do it."

Like most Charlestonians who grew up when Skipper did, dinner was at two o'clock, "when we came in from school. When I was in high school, dinner was over by the time I got in, so there would be a plate for me warming on the stove. We had rice and gravy and fried chicken a lot. On Saturday, we had steak and on Sunday, we had roast beef and rice and gravy. We had a maid who cooked for us. We didn't eat out much, but I do remember eating at Henry's – it had good food. And Robertson's Cafeteria was on Broad Street. But there weren't too many places to eat.

"Mama did the grocery shopping at Rodenberg's on Rutledge Avenue and at the one on Cannon Street where the MUSC parking garage is now. She also went to Harley's Meat Market on President

Street and Harold's Cabin on Spring Street. It was a corner grocery at first but then they started selling specialty items in addition to regular groceries - not just the typical Charleston things. Harold's Cabin finally became part of the Piggly Wiggly on Meeting Street but then just kind of faded away."

Skipper and several of his childhood friends received their college education right where they had grown up - at The Citadel. Of course, when they joined the Corps of Cadets, they lived in the barracks, even though their families lived on campus. Skipper graduated from The Citadel in 1955 with a degree in electrical engineering and went right into the Air Force. "I ended up in communications school and then was sent to Newfoundland. They always send Southern boys north and Northern boys south! In 1957, they had a reduction in force and asked me if I wanted an early out. I said yes and came back to Charleston."

Skipper's father, Arthur Jenkins, Sr., had been a harbor pilot, so some might say it was pre-destined that Skipper would enter the profession. "I got my nickname 'Skipper' at an early age - way before I became a harbor pilot. My daddy was a pilot and I was the little skipper. So when I came back after the Air Force, I went to the Harbor Pilots Association as an apprentice for three years and then worked as a pilot for thirty years. We go to sea and meet a ship coming in. The ship slows down and they put a Jacob's ladder over the side; we climb up and take over the ship. We tell the ship's quarter master how to steer and the speed to go. If a ship is arriving at four o'clock in the morning, we'd leave town at two and go out in our boat and meet the ship. Then the pilot rides the ship into the city. And we'd go the other way – when a ship is leaving port, we leave with them and our boat would be outside the harbor waiting on us. You'd tell them where to meet you – say, 'I'll get off at #3 buoy' or whatever.

"A lot of ships move in and out of Charleston at night. Most ships arrive between midnight and daylight and sail by late afternoon up until midnight. So my phone would ring all hours of the day and night for me to come to work. When I turned sixty, my wife said, 'When can you quit?' and I said now. She said, 'Do it!' I've been retired nineteen years."

The headquarters for the Harbor Pilots Association is on Adger's Wharf near the southern end of Waterfront Park - next to what used to be the Navy's degaussing station. "That place is now a private home. They are selling it and asking a tremendous amount of money. But the harbor pilots still operate from next door."

With the large Navy presence that was here for over sixty years, Skipper says, "We took out Navy ships, too. Many a submarine, but we had destroyers, mine sweepers, tenders – everything. We did all of them."

Hurricanes usually put a stop to navigation for a day or two. Skipper explains, "Merchant ships will usually double up their lines and tie down in port. Navy ships would leave port and try to outrun the storm." But other inclement weather doesn't stop the flow of shipping traffic. "One time in particular, it was freezing cold. I went to the Exxon terminal to take a tanker out to sea. It was a half-mile walk down the dock to the ship, and by the time I got to it, icicles had formed on my eyebrows! There were 40 or 50 mph winds. I got on the ship and really didn't think it would sail. But the captain said, 'Are you ready to go?' I said, 'All the lines are gone so I guess we're ready. Let's go.' A transformer in Mt. Pleasant had exploded and all the lights on the Cooper River Bridge were out. By the time we got outside the harbor, the winds were blowing about 70 mph. The pilot boat was rising about 30 feet on every wave. I had a big guy on deck named George, and he yelled to me, 'What you gonna do, Captain?' I said, 'Next time she comes up, grab me,' and he snatched me off the ladder. We were weightless going down! Then, as we were heading back in, the sea was monumental and he said, 'Captain, what we gonna do now?' That cargo ship I'd just left was going to the (Panama) Canal Zone and I said, 'I don't know any-body down there!' so we beat our way back into town. It took us an hour to get back, but we never really thought about it – it just had to be done. You had to get on and had to get off.

"One of the last jobs I had was sailing from the Wando terminal. You couldn't see because of the fog. They had a Raycon electronic beacon on the bridge that showed the center of bridge, but we never even saw the bridge on the way out. We went out on the radar picking up the buoys."

A while back, Skipper had a knee replacement. They called it 'pilot knee' from climbing up and down ladders. Yet he never fell off one. "We only had one fella fall off a ladder, but it wasn't his fault. There were two Norwegian ships passing and they got so excited waving to each other that they forgot to tie the ladder off. So the pilot and the ladder went overboard!

"Near the end of my time as a harbor pilot, we were supposed to wear a little bubble that was activated with CO_2. If it got wet, it would pop open like a flotation device. But most people didn't use them because they got in the way. If somebody fell over in the middle of the night, you'd never find them. We were jumping off and on ships at three o'clock in the morning."

But there have been some mishaps in the business. Before Skipper became a harbor pilot, "a ship took out the Ashley River Bridge. The story was that the pilot was approaching the bridge going to Coppers' Company up on the Ashley River. He claimed the bridge didn't open on a timely basis and he lost steerage. It ended up with pretty bad damage to the bridge. It was out for a long time and anybody that lived across the bridge couldn't get into town. My in-laws had the Coburg Dairy and they had a boat they ran back and forth into town. Somebody also set up a ferry service that would drop people off in town and then they'd have to walk or get somebody to pick them up."

Skipper was only a child when a ship hit the Cooper River Bridge in the 1940s, but he says that accident had nothing to do with pilot navigation. "A freak storm came up. The ship didn't have any steam on the engines because they'd been anchored there awhile. It dragged anchor and the ship was dragged right into the bridge. We were at my uncle's property on the Wando River and were driving back into town. We had to detour and go up through Highway 41 and around through Summerville."

Locals know that storms are a part of living in the Lowcountry. Skipper says, "We got married during Hurricane Gracie. The storm had actually gone by the time we got married, but we still had a lot of rain. Her father had set up a tent outside in front of their house at the Coburg Dairy. The reception was wet but it didn't seem to bother anybody."

When Skipper retired, his mother commissioned a painting depicting him at Adger's Wharf with a harbor pilot boat tied up behind him. "An artist named Bruce Skidmore painted it. He took about two rolls of film, and I sat for him a couple of times. I had a little more hair then."

Skidmore's portrait of Skipper

Another painting hanging in Skipper's home was given to him by the Harbor Pilots Association. Skipper explains, "The Henry P. Williams, a tall-masted sailing ship, was designed after a Gloucester fishing smack. The ship was used by Charleston's harbor pilots in the early 20th century. The pilot boat left the city at noon on Monday and didn't come back until noon the next Monday. The harbor pilots would sit out there and wait on different ships to come. They had a small boat they put overboard, and a deck hand and an apprentice would row the pilot over to the ship to be brought into port." In the background of the painting is another ship. Skipper says, "She was the Charleston Light and was used as a guide for ships to enter the harbor."

Skipper's life history is reflective of much of Charleston's history - from shrimping in the creek at his family's plantation to time spent at The Citadel and later his role in guiding ships safely into and out of this important seaport town.

And the paintings on his walls help to illustrate the history of both.

A HOME AWAY FROM HOME

Dan Croghan

Dan Croghan was the youngest boy in a family of seven children. But he lived with nearly eighty others when he was growing up. Their home was the Catholic Orphan House.

"I was about five years old when my father passed away in 1941. My mother didn't want to break us up by sending us to live with different relatives, so she managed to get us all in the Catholic Orphan House. The oldest three went in there together at the ages of about six, seven, eight years old. My twin sister and I went in a year or so later, and then my youngest sister went in a year or so afterward. We went in more or less as we started school. The orphan house didn't take younger children; they had enough to worry about than to have babies and smaller ones. When I first went there, I was the youngest boy in the home - the pet. Then along came a boy who was younger than me!"

The home was on the northeast corner of Logan and Queen Streets. It was run by the Sisters of Charity of Our Lady of Mercy, a local community of nuns. However, it did receive some funds from the city and was often referred to as the 'city orphan house.' The orphanage consisted of two separate brick buildings – old houses really – that were each four stories high. The boys lived in one and the girls in the other. The two were connected with large porches in the rear. "I would think the buildings would've made a great movie set for a haunted house," Dan says.

The first floor of Dan's building was used for indoor recreational activities, and each child had a locker there to keep personal belongings. The dining hall was also on that floor. The second floor had the chapel, the study hall, and a community room for the Sisters to use. The third floor was used as the infirmary. Dormitories were on the fourth floor. On that floor, there were four huge rooms, each with about ten twin-sized beds. One nun was assigned to each dorm room and had a portion of the room cordoned off as her quarters. Her privacy was made possible with a curtain surrounding her area. Dan recalls, "When I was older, in the big boys' dorm room, she had a radio and would let us listen to things like the Hit Parade and Sam Spade and a few murder mystery programs. But we'd be in bed by ten with lights out. I remember during the war, there used to be air raid drills when we were sleeping. She'd get us up and we'd all have to go down to the third floor and stay there for as long as it lasted; then we'd all go back to bed."

All the children attended Cathedral parochial school or Bishop England High School. On school days, the boys and girls were in the study hall together from five in the afternoon until six thirty. Then they'd go together down to the dining hall for supper. "After supper, all those kids had to get washed up and a lot of times we'd sit down together and say the rosary. Then we'd go to bed. Nobody ever hung out upstairs at other times; it was strictly for sleeping."

Dan says the home was clean and well-kept. "We had everything we needed. We were well-clothed, warm, and they fed us best they could. Sometime the food didn't taste all that good because they had to cook in such large quantities and had to use powdered milk and powdered eggs during the war. But we weren't hungry and it didn't really taste that bad."

All the children had chores. "Everybody had to pull their weight," Dan explains. "One chore I had was to make up the beds and to clean the floors in the dorms. The floors were wooden so we had to scrub them on our hands and knees – not mop them. Usually, somebody would help you. The duties would be rotated. I don't know how long that lasted, but to me, it lasted too long! I still don't like to make up beds!"

There was paid help that would come in to do the laundry, but the girls also helped with that. "There was a separate building in the back called the laundry. They did a lot of laundry – clothes, sheets and pillows. Girls would also help out in the kitchen. The boys were responsible for other things like raking leaves, but we didn't have that much lawn to take care of – it was mainly dirt. We also had to put coal in the furnace. Occasionally, we might have to change a light bulb or something, but any fix-it things like carpentry were done by people they brought in."

There was plenty of time – and space – for play. "The back yard was a huge lot. We had a basketball court – dirt, of course – and beyond that was an area to play baseball – not a regulation field but it was big enough." And there was no shortage of playmates. "We had all this room to play and all these kids, so the neighborhood boys would come to play. The kids that came were mainly Catholic kids and one Jewish boy who lived across the street. In the summertime, we all stayed right there and played all day."

Dan says that even with forty or so boys in residence, there really weren't too many fights. "Every once in awhile, kids would get in a fight – and both would be punished. There wasn't any physical punishment – maybe once or twice someone got that - but it wasn't all that bad – nothing too severe. However, there were consequences – like having to write 500 times 'I shall not do this.' There was one nun – a little tiny person – who carried a big stick. I don't know if she ever used it, but she did a good job and had control of the boys - and half of them were bigger than she was! There was no rampant rebellion or disregard for authority. Everybody did what they were told, and whatever they did worked."

However, there was no roaming the streets or riding bicycles for the kids at the Catholic orphanage. Dan says, "If you went anywhere away from the home, you needed permission from the nuns because they had to know where you were." But there were several mom-and-pop stores nearby if someone needed something. "Catty-cornered from the home was a grocery store run by a Greek man – Demos. There was another store up on the corner of Logan and Magazine Streets and another as you went around to Beaufain and Coming. And on Queen Street near Franklin Street was another mom-and-pop store. During the summertime, we'd go across to Demos for popsicles because we could get them back to the home before they'd melt."

Dan says it was a peaceful, quiet neighborhood. And at the center of it was the Catholic Church. "All that area belonged to the Cathedral. If you were in the home, you were familiar with all that." The convent was behind the Cathedral, on the southeast corner of Legare and Queen Streets, where there are now modern row houses. The Cathedral School was next to that, facing Queen Street. The Carter-May Home for elderly women was on the side of the lot that faced Broad Street. "There were four or five apartments in there. Miss Marie May took care of that. She was the sister of Father James May who was pastor of the Cathedral and co-founder of Bishop England High School. And the bishop's house was at 114 Broad," two doors from the Carter-May Home.

The children at the orphan house often had additional duties at the church. Dan explains, "They always had a breakfast for the servicemen after Mass on Sunday. I used to have to set up tables and chairs and take them down afterward. I never got to have breakfast there, though!"

"Some of us were altar boys. We'd serve at an occasional Mass in the chapel at the orphan house, but we also served for Masses at the Cathedral. And we'd serve at Mass at the convent every day.

The nuns who worked at the hospital and those who taught at some of the parochial schools lived in the convent. For several years, I had to serve 6:30 a.m. Mass there every day – another boy and I took turns. After Mass, I'd come back to the home and have breakfast before school.

"One year when I was in high school, they were having daily Mass during Lent at Cathedral School, and Father May said the nun who was to lead the prayers wasn't loud enough. So he made arrangements for me to be there and start the prayers. That meant every school day during Lent, I went from serving Mass in the convent at 6:30, then went to Cathedral School to start the prayers, then I went up to Calhoun Street to Bishop England! But there is always a plus - I got out of my first class!"

Dan remembers, "My favorite memory of serving on the altar was Tenebrae. It was a night service right before Easter. There was a big procession and they'd chant prayers - it was all very impressive. The altar boys would get to sit in the sanctuary inside the altar rail. During one part, they'd turn off ALL the lights in church. It would be pitch-black and everyone was supposed to sit and meditate a while. Then the lights would come back on and they'd continue with the service. One night, we little angles were sitting there listening to the chanting, and the lights went out. After a while, we heard something go 'pop!' Well, one of the altar boys had a pea shooter and shot one of the priests in the back of the head! Of course, we had the riot act read to us afterward - and never did find out who did it. But it was funny!

"A big thing was when a new bishop was installed. All the priests were altar servers at that Mass, but two altar boys were chosen to be train bearers for the bishop and archbishop. Another boy and I were chosen! The hierarchy had all these capes and trains, and I held the one for Bishop Russell who was being installed. Someone took a picture of him being led to the chair and I'm behind him carrying the train. He had the picture blown up and put it in the bishop's house in a meeting room. I don't know where it is now."

Another duty Dan occasionally had was to go to the bishop's house on Broad Street to take phone messages. "Four or five priests lived at the bishop's house, and if they were all out at night, that would leave his house unattended. So the duty occasionally fell on me to go and be there if the phone rang."

Time at school, at church, and at the orphan house comprised most of Dan's days growing up. But he says he and his siblings maintained a relationship with their mother. "One Sunday a month, most kids got to go visit their parents. My brothers and sisters and I all went together. My father's sister would come get us, and on the other Sundays, she'd bring my mother to visit us. She would bring us cookies and candy – stuff we didn't get other times. We would also go to be with our mother on Christmas for dinner.

"My mother also bought us most of our clothes. If we needed something – like at Easter - we went to Levy's boys' store where every kid in the city went. The nuns would tell my mother what we needed, and she'd get what she could afford. Of course, I'm sure we got some clothes that were hand-me-downs, too. We probably just didn't know it.

"As time went on, my brothers and sisters and I were able to go visit my mother's family in the country and spend the day. My mother was originally from Blackville, a farm community about a hundred miles from here. It was good to get out and go to the country, but it was a let-down to come back to the orphan house that evening." Dan says he would've rather have stayed longer in the country, but the Sisters had to consider the other kids in the home who didn't get to go somewhere. "Finally, they let us go and spend a couple of weeks or so up there. It was good because we got to do things we ordinarily didn't get to do."

Dan says, "The Sisters had a big responsibility - these women handling all these children. Of course, none of them had children, and for some, this was probably the first time they were ever responsible for kids. They were young women. But they tried to let us do as much as they could. They managed to get us to the beach during the summer. The nuns didn't go but they got chaperones. Buses would come and bring us out to Folly for the day. There would be lunch and all out there for us.

"And every year, we'd have a Halloween party which was sponsored by the McAlister family. We bobbed for apples and things like that. At Christmastime, the Navy Yard would have programs for all the orphanages – ours, the Charleston Orphan House, and the Jenkins Orphanage. Every child would get a gift or maybe even two. It was during wartime, and the kids from these homes probably fared better than other kids did.

"We went to the fair every year, too – somehow or other. I think they let us in for free, but Father May would see that each of us had a dollar - ten dimes – so we could ride ten rides.

"We'd also go to the movies. The Sottile family was a Catholic family who owned all the theaters in town. They issued a pass for the home to use, and we'd all walk there together. The nuns didn't go, but they'd get one of the boys' mothers to take us. We'd line up on Charles Street (now Archdale Street) and walk up to where it becomes St. Philip Street. Then we'd take a right on Beaufain and walk to King Street. The kids behaved and didn't take off running and stayed in the line. Safety was a factor, too. The farthest we walked was the Garden Theater so we didn't have to cross a main thoroughfare (Calhoun Street). The movie would already be started when we got there, and we'd watch from when we came in and then leave when it got to that part again. There was no question about it and we'd all leave together. We got to see the big movies – like the *Three Muskateers* and the war movies.

141

"We used to go to the Christmas parade and to the parade during the Azalea Festival. They'd march us down Queen Street to King to watch it. We'd also go to the Candy Kitchen on King right above Queen Street. It was a little mom-and-pop run by Mr. and Mrs. Deneaux and they made all kinds of candy. They had something called a punch board you'd buy for a nickel. You'd punch out little squares on a cardboard. There were nine punches, and a little pink mint came out with each punch. If you got a white one, you got a prize – a candy bar or something."

Dan says there was a shortage of bubble gum during the war. "You couldn't get it and if you did, you'd keep it in a glass in the icebox and chew it for two months! There was a man who would sell it in a store near the corner of Queen Street – I think the name of the store was Telegas. There was a side entrance and he'd have a long line if he had bubble gum to sell. The line would form around the corner. And you'd only be allowed to buy five pieces."

Some of the kids from the home played in the city football and baseball league at Moultrie playground. Dan played baseball. "We played on teams with the neighborhood kids. When we played teams in other parts of the city, you'd find somebody with a bicycle and ride up there on the handlebars."

At one point, Dan had a bicycle. "There was an attic – storage area – above the laundry building, and I happened to be up in there one day and saw an old bicycle. I asked if I could fix it up and they said yes. I had to clean it up and oil it and had to buy an inner tube. I think my mother gave me some money to do that, so I fixed it up and used it for running errands. I used to go to the bank for the Sisters and had to take papers to the orphanage's board of directors who had an office on Broad Street."

Another stroke of luck fell Dan's way later when he was in the eighth grade. "Horace Heidt was a talent searcher and went around the country looking for talent. He came to Charleston. The custodian at Murray School, Ralph Sigwald, had a great bass baritone voice and sang the 'Lord's Prayer' in the competition. He was selected to be in the finals in Washington, DC. Murray School had a bus or two they sent up there. They had two extra places on the bus and gave one to me! Ralph won, and we came back the next day. But I don't know how I got that seat!"

Dan says that most children at the orphan house lived there until about eighth grade. "I left right after that in 1950. My mother had a job at the Charleston Health Department in vital statistics and eventually managed to get us all out of the orphan house. She took us out piecemeal, like she had put us in, and we all lived on Coming Street near Wentworth for a while. Later, we moved up to King and Sumter Streets."

Reflecting on his eight years spent at the Catholic Orphan House, Dan says, "The experience on the whole was good. You didn't always want to be there because you wanted to be with your mother or father, but that wasn't possible at the time. In hindsight, when I look back, it was a good thing. It kept us together and it was a necessary thing at the time. And they tried to make it as comfortable and livable as possible. I'm glad it turned out the way it did."

He adds, "They deserve a lot of credit."

SLIGHTLY NORTH OF BROAD

Spero Drake

Most Charlestonians remember shopping on King Street in its heyday, but Spero Drake's memory is of living there. "We stayed on King for over thirty years - from the time I was born until 1968. When I was born in 1935, my father had a corner grocery at 209 King Street, on the corner of King and Princess Street, just below Market Street. We lived above the store. An antique store and a small hotel were also in the block, and on the corner of Market and King was a restaurant/bar. That's all torn down now. The Saks store was built in 1995 and took over that whole short block," now called Majestic Square.

But the Drakes had long since left the block by the time that happened. When Spero was about eleven years old, his father moved the business a few blocks down King Street. "My dad didn't own the property at #209, so when the owner decided to sell the building, we opened a grocery store at #129, right next to Tellis Pharmacy. We could sit on the porch above the store and had a perfect view of parades coming down King Street during the Azalea Festival and the Christmas parade on Thanksgiving Day."

Spero says that the area of King – from Broad Street up to Market – was a thriving business district when he was growing up in the 1940s and 50s. "Berlin's was (and still is) on the corner of Broad and King. For awhile, there was a little restaurant/bar a few doors up from it. Poulnot's drug store was in the old wood house, the Lining House, on the other corner of Broad, across from Berlin's, and there was a hair salon next to that." And there were even other grocery stores besides Spero's father's store in the same block. The Panos store was next to Poulnot's. Mazos was across from Tellis Pharmacy, and Marchink's was on one corner of Queen and King. On the corner where the Preservation Society is today was Charleston Florist. Where the parking garage is now, there was a Chinese laundry on the corner, a little cemetery next to it, a dry cleaner, and F.A Bailey's air conditioning. And on the northeast corner of Queen was a liquor store. "During World War II, the man who owned it had a little place in the back where he'd sell candy and bubble gum to kids. Those were tough things to come by in those days."

A little farther up, there was a big apartment complex across from the Drake family's first grocery store. The building had been built in 1889 as a YMCA. "When I was real young, there was a fire there once. My sister was real worried about the fire coming across the street to our place, but I slept through it all." Another bit of excitement came to the neighborhood during the time that Spero's family had their second store. "A man would come to our store to deliver milk and he'd park behind our store. There was a gap – a driveway – between our store and the next building, and he'd use it to get to the parking lot behind our store. One time, he went to leave and pulled out onto King Street but hit the gas instead of the brake. He ran right into Bailey's air conditioning place across the street from us."

Spero remembers that there were a lot of small shops all around the city. But running a small store in those times was a challenge. "All the shops would carry credit - somebody could buy something from us and just put it on the tab. Then, once a month, they'd come pay. But a number of people didn't pay their accounts. And when the automatic groceries came in, they really hurt my daddy's business, too."

Spero's parents had moved to Charleston from Greece before he and his three siblings were born. His father's brother was already living in Charleston and had a grocery store on the corner of Tradd and King. Across Tradd, his aunt ran a beauty parlor. And on the southwest corner was a gas station called the Fort Sumter Filling Station. "It was a residential area except for that corner," Spero explains. "These days, there is a fancy house – built about fifteen years ago - on the corner where the gas station was. I remember that DHEC had to get involved with that property when they were building the house because of the gas tanks buried in the ground."

Spero's uncle later opened a liquor store on Broad Street, right next to the post office. He says, "I'd deliver liquor on my bicycle for him. I used to make deliveries occasionally for my daddy, too. And I had a paper route for the *Evening Post* which, at the time, was on the corner of Meeting and Queen Streets. At one time, I delivered

Spero's uncle's store

telegrams for Western Union which was on East Bay, seven or eight doors above Broad Street. I used to ride all through the downtown streets with my delivery jobs. I enjoyed seeing all the shops and the people while I was making deliveries."

When Spero was a boy, he frequented the usual recreational haunts of other downtown children. "I'd play at The Battery around the cannons and statues. And the Catholic school behind us - back there on Queen Street near Archdale - had swings. I used to play a lot with the black kids who lived on Archdale and back in that neighborhood - ball or whatever. It didn't occur to me until one day when I was older – maybe in high school - that there was a sign for separate water fountains for blacks and whites at Kress. I didn't understand why they were separate.

"I played at Moultrie Playground near Colonial Lake. Sometimes I'd fish in the lake. We'd put bait on a bamboo stick and catch whatever we could. But I wasn't really much of a fisherman. I can also remember climbing out the window of our house above the store and going down to a magazine store on Market Street – where the side entrance to Charleston Place is now - to buy comic books. Felder's barbershop was on the King Street side of that hotel. I used to get my haircuts there when I was growing up. They were all black barbers there.

"I'd ride my bicycle to music lessons at Leonard's School of Music on Meeting Street, a few doors south of Market. Daddy sent me to Leonard's to learn the clarinet. The studio was upstairs above a store. I don't remember what kind of store because I'd just make a beeline there and have to climb up a dozen or so steps to get to the studio. They had individualized lessons but also had the band come together every so often to play for recitals. If you cut up or didn't pay attention, you'd get whacked on the hand by everybody in the band with their belts. I took lessons for about three years, probably until I was about thirteen years old. Mr. Leonard's son and daughter played trumpet and other instruments, too. They were good. After the lessons, I'd go over to a place on Market Street and buy a hot dog with chili. But there wasn't much else in that area."

Spero attended first through sixth grades at Craft School and then Nathan Junior High for seventh and eighth. "It was right next to Memminger High School and was on the same lot. Then I went to Charleston High School which had girls also by that time. Before that, it was just for boys and Memminger was just for girls.

"I walked to school until I got to high school. Then I rode a bicycle. I wasn't too involved in extra-curricular activities, but I was in the honor society one year and played one season of basketball until I had a foot problem. Every day after school, we went to Greek school, so I really couldn't get involved in school activities. I'd come home after school and then about four o'clock take a bus to get uptown to the church. We studied the Greek alphabet, the language, poems. And we'd have plays that the parents would come to once a year."

In those days, the Greek Orthodox Church was on St. Philip Street where the roadbed is now elevated for I-26. It was a small church. "My sister became the organist there when she was just twelve years old! She also played at the Unitarian Church on Archdale Street and at Citadel Square Baptist Church for awhile. As a child, she was taught piano by Miss Hester B. Finger and by Mrs. Lucas who taught the organ. My sister later went to Converse College and studied music."

Spero says that "most of the Greeks lived uptown - on Grove Street, St. Margaret Street, or on Rutledge Avenue. The ones who had grocery stores lived downtown. On the weekends, all the Greek kids went to the movies together and played together. And a good many Greek families owned summer houses out on Folly Beach. My uncle had a beach house there. He would work during the day and then go to the beach at night. The house was on the third street back, but it may be on the second street back now because of so much washing away.

"In the summertime, we'd go out there and go from one house to the other and play 'half rubber.' You used a broom stick to hit the ball. It was hard to hit!" Spero also played softball as a teenager at Hampton Park playground in a church league. "I played for our church. We had a good team. It was a lot of fun and we'd usually go somewhere afterward to get something to eat. Kate's Drive-in was on the corner of King and Spring Street. We used to go there a lot. I loved their fried onion rings! We'd also go to Piggy Park on Rutledge, and the Fork Restaurant, roughly where Wendy's is now on the Crosstown. The Fork was an indoor place with a little bar and two dozen or so tables. I went there a lot.

"Once or twice a year, when I was a child, my dad would take us to Henry's to eat. That was a fancy restaurant. It's still there on Market Street." But Spero says most of the time, his family ate at home. "We were not rich by any means, but having a grocery store, we always ate pretty well."

After high school, Spero attended The Citadel. "I grew up with parents from the old country, and whatever they said, I did. I was the third child - my brother was seven years older. Dad made him go there and he hated it and dropped out before the first year ended. I didn't know what I wanted to do and had been kind of sheltered playing with my brothers and sister and other Greek kids. Engineering was the coming thing, and I was halfway decent in math and chemistry, so I went there. And it was here in Charleston. I wasn't going hundreds of miles away, and it pleased Mom and Dad.

"I wasn't gung ho at The Citadel, but I didn't have the problem that a lot of cadets have. Because of the upbringing I had, it was fine. I did what they told me to do, said 'yes sir, no sir.' The drilling and discipline didn't bother me. I had classmates who would break barracks, and some of them would go around selling ice cream after curfew. But I followed the rules and stayed out of trouble. I never walked a tour (as punishment) in my life."

Spero says he had eight job offers after graduation, but only one was in Charleston. "I ended up going into the Army as an officer. When I came back home after four years, I went to work at the shipyard and learned the practical side of electrical engineering – hands-on. My instruction at The Citadel had been more theory. I worked at the shipyard in the testing department and learned how to check antennae when they installed them on ships. Just before the shipyard closed in the 1990s, I went to work at NAVELEX and was in charge of the SESEF which is right next to Ft. Moultrie. They run checks on ships' antennae and equipment.

"In those days, the only hope you had of a job here was the ship-yard. It was a decent job with benefits. Through the 1960s, the shipyard had many scares about being closed, so I started think-ing about a second income because of the fear of losing my job. I think because of my upbringing and my parents always thinking about security, that has played a large part in many of my deci-sions. There was a big scare in 1972 and they laid off a bunch of technicians. The people at the shipyard were always saying, 'God help us if (Congressman) Mendel Rivers dies.' Well, when he died, I was supporting my mother and raising my niece and nephew, so job security was always on my mind and I got involved in buying rental property. I used to have tenants who'd stay for years, but after Hurricane Hugo, the rental business changed. I would have tenants who would skip out. Everything changed. So I got out of the rental business after forty years."

Spero has been a part of Charleston's annual Greek Festival from its inception and has seen – and helped – it grow into a major event. "The first year, we had a raffle for a trip to Greece and I won it! We've been having the festival for forty years. It started out at Middleton Place. We had only a one-day festival back then and about 1,000 people came, but within ten years, it increased to about 10,000 people. The festival stayed out there for twelve or fifteen years but it became a bit too rowdy with partiers. We moved it to Charles Towne Landing, but Hurricane Hugo came along and destroyed that place, so we were forced to go to Marion Square. I was the supply man and trying to orchestrate the delivery of cookies and ovens and pots and pans by 18-wheelers was a nightmare! But we stayed there until the city decided to renovate Marion Square. Then we started having it at the church. By that time, the church had bought the property next to it on Race Street and had made a park there. At one time, there had been about two dozen small houses there. Our priest lived in one and also, in her later years, my godmother moved into one right next door to our church. About fifteen years ago, the city bought all those houses and moved them over to Floyd Manor and renovated them. So our church bought the property and made the park. That's where we have the Greek Festival every year now on Mothers' Day. It was decided to change it to the fall for awhile, but now it's back to Mothers' Day."

The area of King Street where Spero's father's store was looks a lot different these days than when the Drakes lived there. Among other things, the building that was his father's store has been demolished and a newer building with a law firm is now on the site. Spero remembers, "In my dad's store, there was a crack in the window on one side of the entrance door. We had a lot of hurricanes when I was growing up. Somehow, miraculously, the window – and the crack - survived all the hurricanes!"

But neither the window nor even the building were able to survive the changing times.

HOME AGAIN

Frederick Stuhr

Fred Stuhr grew up at 5 Gadsden Street. "My father built the house in 1937, around the time I was born. There was a vacant lot behind our house and everything beyond it was marsh and mudflats. A tidal creek ran from Colonial Lake under Ashley Avenue and into the Ashley River. Our neighborhood was the western edge of the city."

Out in the marsh, an old ferry boat sat stuck on a mudflat. It was the Sappho, the ferry that had run from Market Street over to Mt. Pleasant, before the Cooper River Bridge was built. Fred says, "We called the marsh 'Sappho Bay.' We had a little wharf that ran out over the pluff mud so we could get to the Sappho. We'd climb all around on it – risk our lives – it was rotting in the mud. The older boys would leave a row boat out there, and we'd row from there out to the beacons in the river and dive off those and go swimming."

Fred says the Sappho disappeared when the marsh was being filled in. "They kept bringing in trash, and that area was called the dump. It was only about a city block - Beaufain up toward Montagu - when I was a kid. But later, they filled in more land and they built the Sergeant Jasper Apartments about 1950. That was a big deal."

Not far away from Fred's neighborhood was the Navy's mine craft base on the Ashley River. "It was at the foot of Calhoun Street. That was a major deal, too. The Navy had some barges there that we used to swim off of. The yacht basin was over there, too."

Fred spent a lot of time in or on the water. "As I got older, I remember going to regattas. Each yacht club would have a dance after the regatta. I didn't have a boat and wasn't a member, but I just went for the parties. We'd go to Savannah, too."

When Fred was a teenager, he was a lifeguard and taught swimming at the municipal pool on George Street. "One of my aunts was head of the Red Cross swimming program, and we trained at The Citadel pool. I met so many different people as a lifeguard. The kids from the Danny Jones playground in North Charleston would come down and we'd teach them to swim. They really appreciated that. Years later, people would stop me on the street and tell me I'd taught them to swim.

"I learned to swim in the river and at the beach. Nobody really taught me. In the summertime, we usually stayed at our grandmother's house on Sullivan's Island for a month or so. It was at Station 28 ½. Those were great times. There were five siblings and we'd play cards and swing on the screen porch. We'd play in the sand under the house - make forts and dig. We'd go down to the beach a couple times a day."

In the city, there was no shortage of children where Fred lived. "There were a good many kids in the two blocks of Gadsden between Beaufain and Montagu. We all gathered and played together. We called ourselves the 'Gadsden Street Gang.' About five years ago, we had a reunion."

Fred also spent a lot of time at the city's playgrounds – "Moultrie and East Bay. We'd go to the buildings there and play cards and ping pong. You got to know the guys at different playgrounds. One boy from Gadsden Street was a tough guy who fought in the Golden Gloves. He forged my parents' signature so I could fight. The kid I fought was from the Catholic Orphanage on Queen Street. He was very good. I wasn't trained at all, so he really battered me around! He beat me, but I didn't quit - and I didn't get knocked down.

"My parents liked the fact I was boxing but thought I needed some lessons. So I went to Mr. Matty Matthews' boxing classes. His great-grandson is Clay Matthews who plays now for the Green Bay Packers. Two of Mr. Matty's grandsons were pro-football players – Clay, Jr. and Bruce – after being All-American at Southern Cal. They were the sons of Matty's son Clay who played for Georgia Tech and San Francisco. Anyway, I went to Mr. Matty's classes because he coached The Citadel's boxing team - which was awesome. His son Dale fought on the team, as did Bill Ohlandt, Harry Hitopolous and Harold Shokes. In those days, The Citadel was in the So Con which was comprised primarily of the University of South Carolina and today's ACC teams – Clemson, Maryland, Duke, North Carolina and North Carolina State. In 1948, The Citadel won the So Con boxing tournament! I went to watch it and was going to box for Mr. Matty when I got to The Citadel, but college boxing died out before I got there. However, I boxed in the Golden Gloves a couple more years."

Fred attended grammar school at Craft School. He then went to Charleston High. Fred says, "It is neat that they kept the facade of that building." The school was co-ed by the time he attended. "There were about five hundred students at the school – a hundred and ten in my graduating class. You knew everybody. I also liked the fact that we had excellent teachers – Mr. Seabrook for math, Mr. Bolger for chemistry. College was a snap after that.

"In high school, I swam and played football and basketball. Those three sports took me through the entire school year. We had a city swim meet at The Citadel pool, but we didn't have it every year. Most of the high schools brought a team, even if it was just a couple of people. And we didn't have any practices because there wasn't a facility for kids to get in shape. So all the races were short races. For football, we combined teams with Rivers and Murray, so there was just one city football team. For basketball, we all had our own teams."

Fred as a cadet

After high school, Fred attended college at The Citadel. "My dad said none of his sons were going any place but The Citadel. My father was a Citadel grad – class of '28 – and a number of the kids I went there with had dads who were there when he was. My older brother went as a vet after he left the Army, and he was in class with me there. Vets went to day classes back then - a lot of Korean vets and a few WWII vets. They made good students. They'd been around a little bit and didn't want to lose out on a career.

"As a freshman, it was rough and I was trying to be perfect. I was terrified I'd get a demerit. Most people really didn't know what it was going to be like until we got there. My other older brother had been a cadet, so I kind of knew what it was like - I knew how rough and strict it was. The first week, we got our uniforms and it was pretty easy. They divided us into companies and taught us how to take a rifle apart. It seemed okay. But then, after that, they laid down the law. Corporals and sergeants were out there yelling at you. 'This is what your life is going to be like!' Every time you walked out of your room, you had to go into brace (attention). They didn't harass us outside the barracks, but there was always somebody to yell at you when you'd come back in. It didn't let up at all until the end of the year – the whole freshman year. Finally, at the commencement parade, they lined us up and recognized the underclassmen.

"Upperclassmen weren't supposed to touch you - maybe somebody would poke you in the chest with a finger - but they would get in your face and yell at you about how you can't shine your shoes and so forth. We had to walk 120 steps a minute in the barracks.

They might make you hold a rifle straight out. They weren't supposed to come in your room during evening study period from 7:30 to 11 o'clock. You didn't have to be studying all that time, but you couldn't go to bed before 9:30. Outside, we couldn't walk in front of the chapel and the barracks – we had to walk behind them. Freshman year was very hard."

Even for upperclassmen, Fred says there were some things that today's students might consider hardships. "We didn't have phones in our rooms and there were only two phone booths in the guard-room for 500 guys in your barracks to use. There were no TVs or computers like now. And we couldn't leave campus. My senior year, I had a couple of passes where I could go out, but you had to wear your uniform and they'd get you even on the outside if it was not on properly. Rules were strict and freedom was very scarce.

"There was a formation for every meal and we marched to the mess hall together. We formed in groups for our classes and marched in formation to go to them. We also had formation for the flag being raised in the morning and coming down in the evening – retreat. Everything was done together. These days, I think they just come and go more by themselves. It is much looser now."

But the life of a cadet in Fred's day wasn't all structure. "There were hops (dances) at Christmas and there was the Ring Hop. We'd wear full dress uniforms and have big-name orchestras. And there were tea dances for the freshmen. Girls from the local high schools would come for those. I went to a few, but they were mainly for boys who were from away. I used to bring boys home on week-ends and for Sunday dinner. When my brother was a cadet, he used to bring ten of them at a time! Sometimes they'd come over even when he wasn't there. One of them was Bud Watts who became president of The Citadel in the early '90s. Another he brought home was John Palms who became president of Carolina. Those were great memories."

A traditional past-time for cadets was hanging out at Big John's Tavern on East Bay Street. "My wife said that, when she was young, she would never date a cadet. Some of the girls thought they were animals – loud and drunk. And I told her, 'Yes, that was us!' We had to be back in at midnight but sometimes we got to stay out until 2:00 a.m. after a football game. We'd go over to Seaside on the Isle of Palms and the Charleston Yacht Club at the yacht basin. You didn't have to be a member to go there. And the Ark – that was up on Grove Street right across from the railroad tracks." The Ark was originally near Wentworth and Meeting Streets. It later opened uptown in a bar formerly known as the Boll Weevil, whose name-sake was the Seaboard Coast Line train that ran from a station nearby. "I remember we'd march from The Citadel to that train depot to catch the train to Orangeburg for The Citadel's game against Wofford on the same week-end the fair was in Orangeburg."

Fred admits, "We actually started going to bars when we were pretty young – I was probably sixteen or so. The laws were not enforced and they didn't make a big deal out of it. There was the Five O'clock Club down on the waterfront when Market Street was full of dives. It stayed open all night. It was rough, with fights down there pretty often. Brownell's was a place on Sullivan's Island where we went in the early '50s. It was right as you came onto the island."

After Fred finished The Citadel in 1959, he served in the Air Force for three years. "I had a degree in electrical engineering and got a commission. I always wanted to come back to Charleston after-ward, but there weren't really many good jobs as an engineer. I could've worked for SCEG or the paper mill, the Navy Yard or the telephone company, but I went to went to work for Cal Tech at NASA's Jet Propulsion Laboratory in southern California. I liked that. In the Air Force, I had met technical people who were from Stanford, Berkeley, MIT - very qualified people. So I went to Georgia Tech for my Master's Degree in Electrical Engineering and afterward went back out there to work. In California, people thought me a curiosity."

Fred says Charleston changed a great deal during the forty-five years he was away. For one thing, "everything used to be closed on Sunday. It *felt* like Sunday because of that. It seemed strange when I first went to California and things were open. In Charleston, the stores and movie theaters were all closed on Sunday. They might open the Gloria and show a movie at five o'clock, but that's the only one I remember going to on Sunday. Downtown on Sunday afternoons was a steady stream of cars cruising down King Street."

Another change is that drive-in theaters were big around Charleston when Fred left here. "The Magnolia was on Savannah Highway; the Sea Breeze was by Shem Creek. The Flamingo was in North Charleston and so was the North 52."

Fred says a positive change, however, and perhaps the biggest change in Charleston may be the end of segregation. "*Everything* was totally segregated when I was growing up - restaurants and all that. It was just accepted by whites. Looking back, it's shocking to me how that system was maintained as rigid as it was for as long as it was. The decision to integrate the schools came down in the '50s, but the Charleston schools didn't integrate until the '60s.

"My parents didn't preach hate and felt sorry for the situation of black people, but it's just the way it was. As a kid, I didn't know any black people except 'the help' at home. I remember one time riding with our maid on the bus when I was about fifteen. When we got on the bus, she went to the back - the first seat in the back - and I sat in the last seat before 'the back.' That was a unique experience, but I didn't really think too much of it."

Fred says he doesn't remember having much contact with black children. "Sometimes, black kids would come to where we were playing at the Ashley River and we'd play together - like throwing rocks in the water - but there was really very little interaction." Fred notices that "today, there is still segregation in churches, for the most part. I think there is just a history there. Martin Luther King said the most segregated time in America was eleven o'clock on Sunday morning."

Fred grew up attending St. Johannes Lutheran Church on the corner of Hasell and Anson Streets. "St. Andrew's was around the corner from it on Wentworth Street, so there were two German Lutheran churches in Ansonborough. St. Matthew's came out of St. Johannes, and St. John's on Archdale is the oldest."

Fred's great-grandfather, Henry Detrich Stuhr, came to Charleston from Germany in 1865. "He was a carpenter and made caskets. From that, his sons, J. Henry and Albert, started the J. Henry Stuhr funeral business. Later, my father and his cousin, Albert, ran the business. Now my brother and my cousin run it. Charlestonians used to say Connelly's buried 'below Broad' people, McAlister's buried Catholics, and Stuhr's buried everybody else.

"My father's mother was also German. Her father was a Viohl and had a feed company in Charleston. The Germans in Charleston integrated themselves into the larger community, and there were a lot of marriages to other ethnicities. My father belonged to the German Friendly Society which had to do with German heritage. On the wall there are inscriptions and pictures of the founders and early members going back to before the American Revolution. Germans were prominent here in colonial days and they supported each other in business. Today, the Friendly is more of a social organization. They have a Stuhr night when the dinner is sponsored by Stuhrs and they recognize my father and his cousin, Albert." Fred says he was once told by a German that "the word 'stuhr' (pronounced shtoor) means 'stubborn,' but that it could also mean 'slow to change one's mind' or even 'slow of mind,' at which the German laughed heartily!"

Fred says he attended a funeral recently and saw many people he has known through the years. "A eulogist talked about how important family reputation is and living up to the name. The thing I enjoyed most about growing up here was the connectivity of family and friends and knowing everybody. When I would bring playmates home, my father would want to meet them and quiz them about their family tree. He knew the family trees of half of Charleston! It had to do with making connections."

For Charlestonians, it still does.

A HEAVENLY CHILDHOOD

Rosemary (Binky) Read Cohen

Binky Read Cohen was born in Charleston and has lived here nearly her entire life. It's no coincidence that is also how long she has been in love with the arts. "We were very fortunate to grow up in a household where my parents loved art and music. It was just part of our lives."

Binky's parents, Joe and Florence Read, were friends of William Halsey and Corrie McCallum, two of the most prominent Charleston artists of the 20th century. "Daddy used to give William a hundred dollars when the Halseys went on trips to the Yucatan or Italy or somewhere. The deal was Daddy would later get a painting that William would've sold for $200. That was back in the days you could get a Halsey for $200!

"I remember once I really wanted to buy one of William's paintings. It was $100. I thought maybe I could pay him $25 a month toward it. While I was anguishing over the financial decision, my mother said, 'What are you going to do with that $25 a month if you don't buy it!'"

Binky has several Halsey pieces that she inherited from her parents or bought on her own. "This one was hanging in the kitchen of our house on Murray Boulevard when I was growing up. It's an early Halsey." She shows another and says, "Here's another early one that is the view at the corner of State and Chalmers Streets. I think a bank is there now but there was a house there at the time. William told Mama and Daddy that, every time they bought one of his paintings, the building in it was torn down!"

Binky shows off paintings by other local artists as well. "This is old St. Andrew's Church. It was done by Ann Karesh – it is lovely. I bought it at an art show on Church Street. They used to have outdoor art shows there in the spring across from St. Philip's Church."

Photographs line Binky's walls, too. "This is my favorite picture of my parents," she says. "It was taken at the Francis Marion Hotel at a party held by the National Council of Jewish Women. Daddy wrote on the back 'To Binky, from your parents, in a most subdued mood.' They clearly were not!"

Binky as a 'coat check' girl at the NCJW event

A large photograph on the wall shows the Read family's store on the corner of King and Spring Streets. Early photos of her father's parents flank the picture. "The store was originally called Read and Dumas. My great-uncle, Mendel Dumas, was my grandfather's brother-in-law. He'd had a store in Bonneau, and Grandfather had a store in Moncks Corner. That was kind of the Wild West back then. In 1912, they opened a store together in Charleston.

"After three years, Uncle Mendel left the store and it came to be called Read the Leader. Then, sometime in the 1930s, Daddy and his brother, Dan, who had been a doctor in Moncks Corner, bought the store from Grandfather and it became Read Brothers. Daddy bought out Uncle Dan in the 1950s."

Binky shows off a few more photographs hanging in her hallway. "This is Daddy in 1923 with the College of Charleston's cross country team. He was the captain of the team." A 1940s-era photo shows her Grandmother Read wearing a long black dress and sitting in a kitchen chair on the sand at Folly Beach.

Binky explains, "Daddy's parents came from Latvia in the late 1800s. They were living in Moncks Corner when my daddy was born. He was actually born in Pinopolis at a place Daddy called a 'laying-in hospital.' They moved to Charleston when he was young. At first they lived on Smith Street - #39 - between Beaufain and Wentworth. Uncle Mendel Dumas and his family lived right next door. Later, Daddy's family moved to the third floor of the store which they made into an apartment. It had an entrance from Spring Street. There used to be an elevator. Daddy told loads of stories about going up and down on it.

"Then, about 1920, my grandfather built the house at 60 Murray Boulevard, between Council and Limehouse Streets. We lived upstairs and my grandparents lived downstairs. It was lots of fun. I don't remember my grandfather, but my brother is four years older than I and he remembers him. I do remember when he died in 1941 because my grandmother was very sad. We continued to live upstairs in that house until 1958 when my grandmother passed away; then we moved into the whole house."

When Binky was growing up, there were still quite a few vacant lots on Murray Boulevard. "There were two next to our house. Our back yard was adjacent to Mayor Morrison's on South Battery. He's the first mayor I remember.

"I think my childhood was magic; we never knew want of anything." But Binky adds, "I don't think we were wealthy and I certainly never felt affluent. I never knew who had money and who didn't in my circle of Jewish girls and boys. The girls all went to the same dress maker – Mrs. Wagner – and it never occurred to me. It just didn't. It never made a difference."

Binky's father worked in the store six days a week. "It was closed on Sunday, but when we were in Sunday school, he'd go and check on everything at the store. Mama helped in the store but, as I recall, she was very 'clubby' and loved to play Bridge. She had a Monday game and a Friday game. Her friends would come to the house and they'd have lunch and play."

Binky's family had a housekeeper who came every day. "She was with my family until my father died in 1999. 'Nursie' was just wonderful. When I think of her hours! She was there by 7:30 in the morning - I woke up to the smells of good breakfast food - and she was there until 6:00. I grew up on rice and gravy, roast, string beans; fried chicken, macaroni and cheese and sivvy (lima) beans. She made the most wonderful okra and tomatoes. And the lightest biscuits! She was really a great baker and she made the most wonderful pies and cakes. She used to cook fish on Friday, but I didn't like fish, so as I got a little older, I'd bribe her to make me something else!

"I remember the vegetable man and the fish man with their carts coming through on South Battery. They'd be yelling, 'We got green beans, snap beans, string beans, okra and toma-a-a-to.' I can just hear him! And we had milk delivered by Coburg Dairy. That Golden Guernsey milk with the cream on top – I used to love that cream! If I was really good, Nursie would let me have a spoonful of that cream."

When 'Nursie' first came to work for the Read family, she lived in a house on the corner of State and Cumberland Streets where there is now a parking lot. "Railroad tracks were across the street. I think Halsey did a painting of that area, and I think my brother has it. There were a number of African-Americans living around there at the time. Years later, when her grandson was grown, he bought her a house on Congress Street. She was in her eighties when Daddy died, but she still came to work every day and fixed his breakfast.

Daddy kept his pills in a dish on the table at home and sometimes he left one. So Nursie would take a cab up to the store to bring it to him and she'd say, 'Mr. Joe, you left this pill.' I was working in the store and would then drive her home to her house. But we didn't go straight home because she always had errands to run.

"Nursie was quite a person. She eventually became a reverend. She was being honored at her church about twenty years ago, and my brother and I went to it. It was wonderful - what they said about her - and I had to get up and say something. It was a beautiful service with all the singing and everything." When Nursie no longer worked for the Read family, Binky says, "I would come to see her every Thursday after I got off from work, and we'd sit and visit in the living room and talk about my sister and brother and my children. When my children were grown, they would visit with her, too. We just loved her; she was just wonderful." Nursie was in her nineties when she died.

"When my grandkids were very small, Nursie was still working for my daddy on Murray Boulevard. The children would sit in the kitchen and she would tell them stories about my son, their father, and how he was sometimes bad. She never spanked any of us but it was a psychological thing. She'd say, 'Go out there and break off a switch for me.' The terror of the switch! I have a photograph of them listening to the stories – they were wide-eyed! She'd tell them, 'That's what happened to him when he didn't listen to me!'

"When we were children and Nursie had to take us somewhere on the bus, I remember sitting in the back of the bus with her. I don't know when I became aware of the injustice. But I do remember the hospital workers' strike in 1969. They marched down to The Battery via Limehouse Street. I actually filmed the march from a window of our house. That was a time when blacks were not welcome at The Battery unless they worked there. When I was very little, Nursie used to take us to The Battery park in the afternoon. All the nurses took the children there. They'd sit on the benches while we'd play."

Binky remembers, "Nursie came half a day on Saturday and every other Sunday. My mother didn't cook, and I didn't learn to cook from Nursie. She'd say, 'Get out of my kitchen.' It was her kitchen! When my grandmother was living downstairs, she had a maid who gave us supper in the evening on Saturday after Nursie had gone home. Mama and Daddy were usually busy socializing in the evening. It was always oatmeal for supper. And on those Sundays when Nursie didn't come to the house, we ate at Henry's (Restaurant). We did that for years and years. I remember Henry's as a wonderful place! I remember my brother always got Boston cream pie for dessert. And somebody must've ordered fish because there was a little container of tartar sauce. My brother loved that. Occasionally, we went to Everett's on Cannon Street, about where Hardee's is now. It was a very good restaurant – regular Southern food. I also remember, sometimes after symphony concerts, we'd go out to eat at a drive-in called The Tower on the corner of King and Grove Streets. But Henry's was our place."

From an early age, Binky's parents fostered their children's talents and interest in the arts. She says, "My parents loved the arts, and frequently we went to see performances at the Footlight Players and the Dock Street Theater." She points to two African-type masks hanging on the wall. "I made these. I took art lessons from Faith Murray when I was around ten or eleven. My father paid for art and piano lessons for us.

"My brother and sister and I all took piano lessons from Hester B. Finger at 166 Broad Street. First we took from Gertrude Cappelman on Rutledge Avenue, right below Cannon Street. I remember the day Mama went to see Miss Finger. I had to stay in the car and said, 'What are you going to do?' and my mother said, 'I'm going to see a man about a horse' which was an old saying like

'It's none of your business.' But I thought, 'Oh we're going to get a horse?' From then on, my brother and I took lessons from her; my sister took from Martha Laurens Patterson who was very involved with the beginning of the Charleston Symphony Orchestra. I think back on how lucky we were that music was a part of our lives. My mother came from a poor family in Aiken, but she also took piano lessons as a child. She told me that she only had two dresses. She'd wear one to school one day, and my grandmother would wash it and she'd wear the other the next day. They were very poor but she took piano lessons."

Binky's three children took music, too, and her son and his wife are both professional musicians. So are his children. Binky says, "I play very little now, but my brother has a degree in music from Harvard. He's always composing." Hanging on her wall is a photograph of her brother with Artur Rubinstein at the Mills House Hotel. Rubinstein performed in Charleston in 1971 at the Gaillard Municipal Auditorium.

When Binky was nine years old, she went away to Camp Watitoh in Pittsfield, Massachusetts with her friend who lived on Gadsden Street. She says, "One of the extra things offered through the camp was to go to Tanglewood (for the Boston Pops summertime concerts) and to see Leonard Bernstein (conductor of the New York Philharmonic). We also went to Jacob's Pillow for the famous dance festival."

Binky remembers as a child going to hear the Charleston Symphony Orchestra perform at Memminger Auditorium. "At intermission, all the men and women who were dressed to the nines were out on the portico smoking cigarettes – the smoke would be swirling around. I was about eight or nine when I started going - when J. Albert Fracht was the conductor. We went to the Community Concerts also where there would be special visiting orchestras and soloists. Mama took us to Columbia, too, because they got more famous musicians there. Mama would pick me up from school, and Miss Finger and Mrs. Patterson would be in the car. We'd go up there and have dinner and go to the concert and drive back home. That went on for a couple of years. One time, we had a flat tire coming back about midnight. Fortunately, a car came and the man changed the tire. That was the last time we went to those. But music was always part of our lives. That was the family part of growing up here."

Binky remembers doing all the usual 'kid-things' as well. "We skated at the indoor skate place up on King Street, a building across from the John Dart Public Library. And we went skating at Folly Beach. There was a rink there right when you came over the bridge – on the right. And on the corner of East Arctic and Center Street, there was a bowling alley.

"When I was ten, Daddy bought a house on Folly Beach - 703 East Arctic. So we were at the beach all summer from the time right after school was out. We stayed upstairs and there was an apartment downstairs.

"Childhood was just heaven; I didn't have a care in the world and it felt so safe. I'd sometime go to the Riviera Theater and walk down Market Street to Meeting to catch the bus home – alone. And there were bars and tattoo parlors along in there! A filling station was on the corner of Market Street where the Wells Fargo bank is, and Hornik's was across the street. It was a wholesale house. Sometimes after Daddy picked us up from Sunday school, we would go there and buy ladies' cotton undershirts and stockings and all sorts of things like that for our store.

"When I was twelve, I started working at the store on Saturdays – if you call it work. I served customers. I think families who own businesses expect their children to help. Later, I remember I'd meet my girlfriends for lunch at Onslow's on King Street across from the Gloria Theater. It had a lunch counter. Then we'd go to the movies."

Even when she was very young, Charleston was safe enough for Binky to walk places. "For my first three years of school, I attended Craft School on the corner of Legare and Queen Streets. I walked from my house every morning to my friend's house at 10-A New Street, and we walked to school together. Then, in the fourth grade, I started Ashley Hall School. Daddy drove me then. Every year, Ashley Hall had a wonderful festival called Kettle Drums. It was a really fun thing. They had games and a dance at night and a water ballet. One year, Mama dressed my sister with a tea kettle hat tied with ribbons, and she carried a drum. 'Kettle Drums.' There was a picture in the newspaper of her wearing it. There was also a song we sang. I can remember some of the song.

"There was a swimming pool at school and we took swimming classes. I learned ballroom dancing at South Carolina Society Hall on Meeting Street. I was the only Jewish child in my class at Ashley Hall, and I became friends with girls who were not Jewish. In the ninth grade, I met a whole group of girls and boys from the Temple and the Jewish Community Center, and we became fast friends."

Binky has been a life-long member of Kahal Kadosh Beth Elohim Synagogue on Hasell Street. "I was at a function there recently, and I looked around at the people, most of whom I don't know, and said to a friend, 'There is nobody else here tonight who has been a member as long as I have!'

"My grandmother and grandfather were Orthodox and belonged to old Brith Sholom Shul on St. Philip Street. I guess he was less Orthodox than many because he had the store open for business on Saturday. But my grandmother kept kosher. She worked in the store and would catch the bus home on Saturday. But on Rosh Hoshana and Yom Kippur – the high holy days – she stayed at the Francis Marion Hotel, as did many Orthodox Jewish people, and they'd walk the block and a half to the synagogue on St. Philip Street. I used to occasionally go with her, but Mama and Daddy belonged to KKBE."

The Read family's store has been a landmark on King Street for over a century. "We sold beautiful material for draperies and upholstery. The shelves were full! Mama decorated many a house. Also, the dressmakers would come in for the material for spring dance recitals at Miss Trudy Oltmann's and Cecilia Vaughn's dance schools. We would get the fabric together for them - sequins and netting and feathers and fringe for 1920s costumes. And taffeta and satin. I remember two satin fabrics in particular - white with red hearts and white with shamrocks."

Binky says that in the mid-20th century, the customers who came in during the week were mostly from downtown, and those from the country came in on Saturday. "Read Brothers also did a good Christmas business. We sold beautiful Effanbee dolls – gorgeous. And I remember when we sold ladies' dresses in our store."

Electronics became a part of the store's inventory in the 1950s. "My brother – who already had a degree in music from Harvard - went to Trident Tech and took classes for electronics and graduated with a degree in it. He wanted to sell musical equipment and to know what goes into it.

"Today, we also sell beautiful bedspreads from India which some people use as tapestries or wall hangings. We sell oilcloth for tablecloths. And lots of acrylic velvet for cars and boats as well as fabrics for upholstery and slip covers. We also have Haitian art and a wide variety of gift items."

Locals know that Read Brothers is still the place to go for notions, fabric and a plethora of hard-to-find items. But there were more than a few other stores on Upper King Street that weren't lucky enough to survive the retail exodus to the suburbs in the 1960s and 70s. "Banov sold work clothes and they also had a pawn shop. There was a shoe store, a radio repair shop, the Army-Navy surplus store, Altman Furniture, Sloan Dry Cleaning, and Leon's Men's Wear. There were a lot of Jewish stores that are now gone."

Downtown on King Street, Binky remembers shopping at Kerrison's. "I remember how they would put the money in those carriers and it would shoot up to the office upstairs. They were kind of like the bank has at its drive-in but they was smaller. I'd love to have one of those containers! And next door to Kerrison's was Snelgrove's and Daisy Bogin. Mama shopped there. The ladies were all dressed up. I think about how those ladies all wore girdles in the summer!"

Binky continues, "Across from the Riviera Theater was Belk, J.C. Penney, and Efird's all on that block where Charleston Place is now. M. Dumas and Son was on the other corner across Market Street. In the next block going down King was Rugheimer's, a tailor shop, and Schindler's Antiques. Herman Schindler and his sister, Mary Singer, ran it. That was a wonderful store. My brother used to go there. He bought old mechanical banks from them. Across the street was the beautiful Birlant's Antiques which is still in business."

Another fond memory Binky has from earlier times is of "so many nice doctors. Dr. Rhett was our pediatrician. His office was on the ground floor of a big house on Rutledge Avenue. Then I went to Dr. Coleman who was a lovely man, too. I had my tonsils out when I was about five, and Dr. Hope was my doctor. That was in Baker Hospital." The former hospital has now become condominiums.

The Fort Sumter House is another example of conversion to condos. "When it was a hotel, Best and Company had a showroom there twice a year. They were an upscale clothing store in New York. In the 1940s, they went to different cities and had catalog shows."

Binky remembers a few other hotels that are now gone. "The Timrod Inn was on Meeting Street, across from Washington Park. The St. John's Hotel was in that block also and was torn down for the Mills House to be built. The Charleston Hotel on the corner of Hayne and Meeting and was torn down for the Heart of Charleston Motel to be built. Now a nice Bank of America building is there." But one hotel that is still with us is the Francis Marion. "I had a 'Sweet 16' dance in the Gold Room there. The Buddy Shaw Band played."

A walk into Read Brothers store is a walk into Charleston's past. Binky says, "Daddy worked in the store until just a couple of months before he passed away in 1999. He loved his work and he loved the store."

She adds, "And I can't imagine a better place to have grown up than in Charleston in the late 40s and 50s. I had a wonderful childhood."

JUST ADD WATER

Gaillard Dotterer

Gilly Dotterer has spent his life soaking in all that the Lowcountry provides an outdoors enthusiast. "We lived in the city but a lot of my mother's family lived on Wadmalaw Island, so every summer, we moved to Rockville. I swam, went crabbing, gigging - we called it graining, striking, sticking. I was a creek man – still am. My sister always wanted us to rent a house at the beach on Sullivan's Island for a month, so we had to do that, but we spent the rest of the time at Rockville. Most of my summer – and my fishing and shrimping - was done down at Rockville."

Even in the city, Gilly found plenty of activities for a young sports-man. "Over where Lockwood Drive is now, there were salt water myrtles, and birds used to nest in them. We'd collect bird eggs. We'd take a spoon and get an egg out of a nest and come home and blow it out. We'd put it in a case. I had about fifty-two kinds of eggs. We also used to hunt ducks right off a sewer pipe that ran between the Sergeant Jasper Apartments and the river. One time we got run off because we were raining some (bird) shot on the building down there where the Coast Guard was.

"We would go fishing, too. Several boys would pick me up on The Battery wall and we'd go out and catch trout. Then we'd go sell them to the fish market on President Street to get money to buy beer. We were wholesalers! In March and April, the water was still too cold for the bait shrimp, but the water coming out of that same sewer pipe was warm and the shrimp would congregate around there. So we'd catch shrimp there for bait. But you'd have

175

to put the shrimp net over your arm when you were casting it - you weren't about to hold it in your teeth, since it had been in that sewer water!"

Often on Sunday mornings, when his friends were attending church, Gilly's father would take him to Medway Plantation in Berkeley County for a day of deer hunting. "Mama taught Sunday school at Grace Episcopal Church, and Daddy and I would go hunting. We'd miss out on church. Mama used to give us a fit!"

Gilly remembers his father telling him about hunting as a boy on his relatives' property West of the Ashley, the land that is now the subdivisions of Springfield, Canterbury Woods, and Providence Commons. "Years later, the place came up for sale and Daddy was going to buy it to hunt on. But he said he walked through the property and it was not like he remembered it. The big beautiful woods were gone and there were a lot of dredge cuts – canals - where they mined for phosphate. We were connected to the Hanahans who were big fertilizer people. They had a fertilizer business and were mining phosphate there for fertilizer production."

Land that had belonged to Gilly's mother's family also has a new identity these days. "They had a beautiful plantation out on Edisto Island which is now Botany Bay Plantation," a 4,000-plus acre heritage and wildlife preserve managed by the SC Department of Natural Resources. The property is open to the public. Gilly's family owned it through the 1800s until the 1930s. "I've got papers and books that tell me about it, but I am not that interested in all the details."

Gilly's parents were members of the Carolina Yacht Club, so sailing was another outdoor recreation for him. There were four teams locally – the Carolina, Mt. Pleasant, Wadmalaw, and Charleston Yacht Clubs. "They still have their annual regattas on the same weekends they used to. Charleston Yacht Club has one at the beginning of July; Carolina has theirs toward the end of July; and Rockville's is the first weekend of August."

Gilly's parents lived on the corner of Council and Gibbes Streets when he was born. The family moved to 16 Atlantic Street when he was five. The house is on the northwest corner of Church and Atlantic Streets. "At one time, it was an A&P grocery store. The Pelzers had converted it to a private home, and when they put it on the market, Daddy snapped it up. My father was an engineer and he said it was good construction – brick and steel – very well built. It is a nice house. My father always used to say, 'This is a rich man's house' because it had all the modern conveniences and the bills to heat it!"

The first school Gilly attended was Mrs. Watts's School. "She had a little school in a building in back of her house on Broad Street. The school went through the third grade, but there were just two classes and everybody was in one of those two rooms. There were about twenty to twenty-five children total. She had another teacher there, too – Miss Mary Lee Hague."

From there, Gilly went to Gaud School which, at the time, was on the corner of East Bay and Tradd Streets. "It was on the ground floor of a big house, right before you get to Rainbow Row. Mr. Gaud had fourth through eighth grades there in one room. He'd be teaching one group and the others would be studying. Then, when Mrs. Watts's son, Berkeley Grimball, came out of the service, he helped Mr. Gaud. He even took it over for awhile, and the school got bigger. They had three or four teachers then, and it moved across the street and later to Broad Street." Eventually, it merged with Porter Military Academy.

When Gilly was thirteen, "my mother and father decided I had to go to the Episcopal High School in Alexandria, Virginia. I went there for two and a half years, then to Christ School in Arden,

North Carolina for a year. The happiest day of my life was when they let me come home and go to Charleston High for my last year. I'd been away a good while and was sure glad to get back to Charleston!"

He adds, "They also sent me to camps. I hated all that, too. Today, I keep telling Mama, 'Y'all were trying to get rid of me!' I went to Kanuga several times. They also sent me to Camp Carolina in Brevard. It was a nice sporting camp, but I hated every minute of it! Get me to Rockville and give me a shrimp net!"

When he was attending Charleston High, Gilly would rather be fishing after school than doing anything else. "We didn't hang around in a crowd. We might go to Piggy Park up on Rutledge Avenue or something at night, but we went fishing during the daytime."

When he was younger, Gilly and his friends hung around Schwettmann's Drug Store on the corner of Tradd and King. "We'd also play sports on the horse lot on Chisolm Street. Sometimes we played at East Bay Playground. It was sort of the meeting place. It's now called Hazel Parker Playground. She was the director there and kept those kids in line."

Gilly says they rode their bicycles and skated everywhere. But they also played closer to home. "I look at those little yards now and see where we used to play Kick the Can and football. My neighborhood was a great neighborhood! We knew everybody. A good many children were probably three or four years younger than me, but six or eight were my age. I don't see too many kids there now. Nobody knows anybody, and probably three quarters of the residents aren't Charlestonians. Who can afford a house downtown these days unless they inherited it? And even if they did, the taxes and insurance costs are so high because you have to pay the replacement value."

As a child, Gilly says he wasn't particularly interested in annual events like the parades during the Azalea Festival and Christmastime. But he does recall some Halloween traditions. "On Lenwood and Limehouse Streets, there were some empty lots with fallen-down trees. The older boys would drag them out into the street and light them on fire. We were younger and couldn't handle all that. But there was a bus stop on the corner of Limehouse and South Battery, and when the bus pulled up to the stop, the driver had to open the doors, whether anybody was on the bus or not. We'd hide in the bushes and throw a two-inch firecracker into the bus! We weren't looking for any candy treats on Halloweeen night, but that was the trick. We'd give those buses a fit!"

Gilly wasn't one to go to the fair either. "But once I went with one of my friends and his parents. I really enjoyed it! As we were coming out, there was an organ grinder with a monkey. I went to pat the monkey, and he bit the hell out of me! I don't remember how I got bandaged up - whether they took me to the doctor's office or to the hospital – but I came to school the next morning with a bandage on my hand. Mr. Gaud said, 'What happened to you?' and I said, 'A monkey bit me.' He popped me one time right in the face and sent me home. I'd obviously been a smart-aleck during my entire career at Gaud School, and this sent him over the top! He was eighty years old or something by then, too. When I got home, Mama said, 'What are you doing home?' and I told her. She called Mr. Gaud and he was to be at our house right after school for her to have it out with him. Daddy and I both heard that Mr. Gaud was coming, and Daddy immediately went back to work and I immediately hauled up the street. Both of us were scared to death of Mr. Gaud."

Gilly's father was an engineer and was involved in the early restoration of Rainbow Row in the 1940s with local preservationist, Mrs. Dorothy Porcher Legge. He was also involved in the construction of several buildings in the city. "My father did the Medical University, the Sergeant Jasper, the Darlington Apartments (now called Floyd

Manor). One time, Daddy said the city fathers called him in for a meeting and told him the Jasper was settling. He told them it couldn't be because they'd broken pile drivers when they hit marl trying to get those foundations in there. Come to find out, it was the sidewalks that were settling!"

Gilly's father also did some work for an insurance company after Hurricane Hazel slammed Myrtle Beach in 1954. "Daddy said the houses there fell because the surf undermined the houses. He was sick over it because those people lost everything. They didn't have flood insurance in those days." But Gilly says the only thing he remembers about hurricanes when he was a kid was that "we'd get those ones with about 70 mph winds and we'd go out there on Low Battery (Murray Boulevard) and take a plywood board and skim-board along the street where the spray was coming over the wall. How our parents let us do that, I'll never know! But there was really nothing major. The only big hurricane I remember was Gracie in 1959. I was in the Army and I tried to call my mother from Germany. Back then, the long distance operator would take your call and tell you she'd call you back when she reached your party. But it was two weeks before she called me back! When she finally did, I asked my mother, 'How are you doing!' and she said, 'We're doing fine. How are you doing?'" Obviously, the city had recovered very quickly from the storm.

Gilly had joined the Army after he attended Clemson for two years. "Most of the Charleston families went to Carolina, but I went to Clemson to study engineering like my father had. My grades there weren't top of the line, and they were about to tell me I'd be drafted, so I volunteered. I was sent to Germany. It was a damn good experience."

After he was discharged from the military, a friend of his mother talked him into going into the insurance business and then the brokerage business.

"One year, I bought a shrimp boat, and it made me more money that year than the brokerage business did. So I decided if one is good, two is better, and I bought another shrimp boat. I left the brokerage business and, for two years, even ran out on the boat myself. I had my sons work for me in the summertime. I made them work out there with those nets and shake out all that hot jelly. Hot jelly floats around on the ocean, and the nets fill up with it and you have to shake the nets out. It's not the same as jelly fish but it does sting. They'd come to me and say, 'We got stung!' and I said, 'I'll show you how to do it.' Well, it burnt me up, too! So I put foul weather gear on and took care of it. It was a good experience for them and it taught those boys they never wanted to be fishermen."

Gilly says, "Fuel cost went up dramatically in the 1970s and I took a beating. I had my two boys up at the Episcopal High School – the same one I hated – and I said, 'I better get out of this and get into something I know.' So I sold the boats and went back into the insurance business."

Gilly says his sons loved the boarding school that he had hated. "I just didn't like it, so I ran away! Another boy from Charleston and I just took off. We knew our parents would be watching the plane or train, so we took the bus back to Charleston. He had a 16-foot boat with a 33 horsepower Evinrude, and we were going to get that boat and live on Kiawah for awhile. Once the bus got to Charleston, we called a friend up and said, 'Come get us!' When we saw his car coming up King Street, we said, 'We are scot-free now!' But damned if the father of another boy who had squealed on us came along in a big old Cadillac and said, 'Get in here, boys.' That was in the day when you respected your elders and did what other people's parents told you to do. So we got in his car. When we dropped the other fella off at his house, his father immediately put him in their car and they took off for Virginia. My parents and I talked about it for awhile, but I still had to go back and work off the 100 demerits I received."

When Gilly was younger, his family typically ate the traditional two o'clock dinner every day after school. "Daddy came home from work to eat but then he went back to work afterward. Some men had a drink and took a nap after dinner, but my daddy wasn't inclined to do that." As for the food, Gilly says, "We generally ate fish on Friday and liver sometime during the week. And something over rice. Or roast beef and macaroni and green beans – that's pretty hard to beat. I love shad roe and grits and salmon – we'd have that for supper in the evening. Mama had all that planned out with our cook."

Gilly says that if his family ate out, it was at the Carolina Yacht Club. "We ate there a lot after church on Sunday. I remember, too, that they used to have slot machines in there. All the clubs did. The women used to get on those things - but not my mother. They took them out in the 1960s. They stuffed them up a chimney and concreted them in. I guess they were thinking they might want to break them out again one day! They really used to pay for the club. But the only other restaurant where I remember eating was The Flag which was on the first floor of the Sergeant Jasper. They moved years later, maybe to the Colony House, and I think still called it The Flag. I remember going there and eating a hamburger-steak with my girlfriend's family."

Like most young children, Gilly and his friends went to the Majestic Theater for the double-feature westerns and the cartoons. "We'd spend the afternoon there, and on the way home, we'd stop for a Chilly Bear at the Candy Kitchen on King Street." But other than that, Gilly didn't spend much time on King Street, since his mother generally shopped for his clothes. "I didn't have to go with her. Every now and then, I had to go to one of the Krawchek stores. But one time when I was in seventh or eighth grade, there was something going on at St. Michael's Church and I needed a pair of gabardine pants. My mother gave me ten dollars to go buy a nice pair. I went to a place way up on King Street called 'Mike, Sam and Jake's' and bought a pair of gorgeous green pants with leopard skin pockets. The pants were pegged (narrowed) from the knee to the ankle. I think I thought they were cool, but it was way out of line! She was very angry."

These days, Gilly says, "I know very few people who still live downtown. My heart is still in the city, but I don't want to live there anymore." He's also given up sailing. "I sailed until the last twenty or thirty years – regattas and even some offshore sailing. I used to love sailing but don't care about it much anymore."

Gilly's favorite past-time

But it's unlikely he will ever give up his love of the outdoors. "My mother's family inherited that land out there on Wadmalaw, and they've had it a lot of generations. It was nothing but a jungle when my grandfather gave it to my parents. I built a house out there over twenty years ago."

And there is plenty of water out there to keep him occupied.

SOUTH OF BROAD
Magdalen (Missy) Siegling Blocker

Missy Siegling Blocker says that when people hear her maiden name, they say, "Oh, I remember going to Siegling Music House and listening to records!" In the music store, there were booths - little glassed in rooms - where customers could listen to a record they were planning to buy.

But, Missy says, the truth is that her father didn't have anything to do with running the business. "My father was a doctor. He was in private practice and was also the head of the orthopaedic department at the Medical College for over thirty years." Dr. John Siegling was also well-known for his work with the Crippled Children's Clinic, later known as the Charles Webb Easter Seal Center.

Dr. Siegling's great-great grandfather came to Charleston from Germany by way of Paris in 1819. Missy explains, "He was a musician and established Siegling Music House. In my lifetime, all the family members owned stock in the business, but one family member managed it. It closed in 1970 when none of the relatives stepped forward to take over that responsibility."

Today, the building that was Siegling's is the site of the Daughters of St. Paul Catholic Bookstore on the corner of King and Beaufain Streets. Missy says, "You can still see the name 'Siegling' at the top of the building. There was a piano show room on the second floor, and they even had an auditorium upstairs. I remember we'd go upstairs to watch the Christmas parade come down King Street – a bird's eye view! On the first floor, they sold music books and sheet music and records. As you walked in the front door, there was a large model – around three feet high - of the RCA Victor dog."

Missy grew up in a Charleston single house at 80 Tradd Street, between King and Meeting. Her mother also had grown up South of Broad. "I don't even know how far my mother's family goes back in Charleston. My grandmother was a Marshall. My grandfather was named Haskell. Both of their families were here for generations.

"We went to St. Michael's Church, although my father was a member of St. John's Lutheran. My mother and all her ancestors were members of St. Michael's. One of my ancestors was the rector at one time. St. Michael's was a big part of my life growing up. I was in the children's choir and the Young People's Service League. I have pleasant memories of St. Michael's, but I married a Methodist minister, so now I have been Methodist longer than I was an Episcopalian!"

Missy made her debut into Charleston society after high school, just as her mother had done. "I wasn't asked if I wanted to - it was expected. I was a reluctant debutant because I was shy, but it was fun."

Missy explains, "Back then, it was done in families who had been in Charleston a long time. The idea of being a debutante, as I understood it, was that you had become an adult, so your parents presented you to their friends. A debutante was presented at an afternoon tea dance or at a ball. It was the family's choice, and sometimes several families would have them together. But my debut was just for me – it was a dance at Hibernian Hall. Each debutante wore a white dress at her party. Emmett Robinson (founder of the Footlight Players) was a good friend of my uncle, and he made my dress. Because my nickname is Missy, he came up with the theme of my being a 'Southern Belle.' My dress had a big hoop skirt, and I carried a fan and wore camellias in my hair."

Debuts in Charleston usually took place during the Christmas season after a girl's graduation from high school. Missy was a freshman in college when she made her debut. "There would be twelve or fifteen girls coming out each year, and you'd attend parties for each other. You could be invited to a couple of parties a day - maybe go to a tea dance in the afternoon, then a ball that night. And perhaps your parents' friends may have a cocktail party where you'd be the honored guest, or someone may have a tea in your honor. My grandmother gave a tea to present me to her friends, and she said afterward, 'Oh, this

Missy as a debutante

was wonderful – I didn't know so many of my friends are still living!' The group of debutantes my year was a small group, but we spent Thanksgiving weekend and most of Christmas vacation going to parties. Part of the fun was having a lot of pretty party dresses!"

Missy acknowledges, "I had nothing to do with the planning. Each mother would make the list of whom to invite. She would also assign a date for each girl who was invited. So, in your invitation, there was a card saying who your date was - you didn't have to worry about who was taking you. For one party I attended, I was assigned a boy who was seriously dating somebody else. I didn't know what to do about it, but we let it stand. He was a good sport about it."

Missy says that the custom of making a debut is "altogether different now. People move so much these days that it's changed. Apparently, it's now what circles you're in. Back then, it was more the old families - being old Charleston meant more. During my year, there were triplets who came from somewhere else and none of us knew them, but they had grandparents from Charleston so they were presented here. My sister lived in Virginia, and both of her daughters made their debuts in Charleston. When I was in college at Duke, a friend from Winston-Salem made her debut there - her family was an old family there."

When Missy began school, she attended Mrs. Watt's School at 170 Broad Street. "In recent years, someone made the statement that it was kind of like a Montessori school – you had a group of students sitting in one room doing their work, and another group was being taught in the same room. When I was in third grade, Mrs. Watt's son, Berkeley Grimball, came back from the war, and he'd take the boys into her kitchen to teach them."

Mrs. Watt's School ran from first through third grade. Then, from fourth through eighth, Missy attended Charleston Day School. "At the time, it was on Elliott Street, on the corner of Bedon's Alley. The building is gone now and a new house has been built there. The school was a classic style 'double house' with four rooms on each floor. Each room was a classroom. It was a pretty building; I realized that even as a child. A nice big play area was in the back. There was an enormous joggling board and a big oak tree where the girls would get together and skip rope and play games. Very pleasant memories.

"There were probably ten or twelve students per class, and in mine, about half were girls. A couple of them were already students there before I got there, since the school ran from first grade to eighth. Occasionally, children of Navy officers would come for a year or two."

Missy says, "The teachers that stand out in my memory are Miss Tenney, Miss Stuart, and Miss Wilson. Miss Tenney and Miss Stuart founded the school in 1937. I also remember the French teacher – Madame Gilbert. It was an excellent education in such a small school setting."

All five girls from Missy's eighth grade class then went on to Ashley Hall. "It was a big school – or at least it seemed like it after Charleston Day! And it was rather intimidating at first. I think there were thirty-eight in my high school graduating class, so that's really not that big! There were still boarding students at Ashley Hall when I was there. I was close to one of them, and I still stay in touch with her."

Missy was a member of the dramatic club and performed in all the Shakespearean plays. She adds, "I was also in the Red Choir for the Christmas play." Since the school's founding in 1924, the play, known as the "Chester Cycle," has been an annual tradition. The play's origin dates to Medieval England and the Nativity of Christ is depicted in episodes. Missy explains, "The choir is dressed in red robes and is on stage during the entire pageant. We were there as part of the scenery and sang between acts."

Missy attended acting classes at the Footlight Players Workshop on Queen Street. "I was in 'Our Town.' I also ushered at Footlight plays and at the Community Concerts at Memminger Auditorium. I can remember going early to fold the programs. The concerts were put on by the Charleston Concert Association, as it's called now. My father was president of the board of directors and was also president of the Footlight board at one time."

Missy took piano lessons "from Marguerite Inman Siegling, a cousin. I walked from Tradd Street to her house on George Street. Even when I was younger, I'd walk everywhere. I'd walk to Mrs. Watt's School - up the south side of Broad Street and cross the street at the Cathedral where there was a crossing guard for the children from Craft School. Then I'd walk the rest of the way up the north side. Sometime, I'd walk with other people but often I walked by myself. Back then, children got lots of exercise going to activities that today someone has to drive them to!"

But most of Missy's world was in her own neighborhood. "Almost everything I did was South of Broad. All my friends were right there. One friend lived in an old Charleston single house on King Street with a big yard next to it - that was the neighborhood gathering place. When we got old enough, we went to the East Bay playground. Hazel Parker was good at getting everyone involved. We had dances and track meets and we'd play cards. When I was a teenager, a friend and I would work the canteen there.

"When we were small, my friends and I would go to the Battery and climb on the statues and cannons. You're not allowed to climb on the cannons now, but we'd be all over them. On the East Battery side, there are two or three big cannons close together. We'd get under them and play house.

"What I really remember about the neighborhood were the corner grocery stores. There was one on the corner of Tradd and King that was owned by Mr. Drake. I have wonderful memories of that store! My mother would give me a couple of dollars, and I'd be sent down there to get milk or whatever was needed. I didn't even have to cross the street because it was in our block on the same side of the street. The store later became Schwettmann's Drug Store. They had a soda fountain and I'd spend a lot of time there, too. Across from it was a beauty parlor. I got my first haircut there. When I was old enough to cross Meeting Street, I could walk down Tradd Street to another corner store directly across from First Scots Church. I remember there were apartments upstairs from it."

Another great thing about Missy's neighborhood is that both of her grandmothers "lived right there. I was fortunate to have them both close-by. I spent a lot of time with them. My father's mother lived across the street from us - #79 Tradd. We were in and out of that house all the time. It was a big Victorian house – a long narrow house. She didn't use the living room much – I remember it was always dark. She lived on the first floor and had boarders living upstairs. There was also a garage apartment which she rented out. That is still there, but the house was torn down when the property was sold to First Scots Church. There is a parking lot now where her house was."

The house where Missy grew up was her maternal grandmother's house. She has a framed sketch of that house – a traditional Charleston single house. "Granny bought the property in 1942. When she bought it, the two-story brick kitchen house in the back had been damaged from the tornado in 1938. I remember half of the roof was gone! It was during wartime and houses were hard to come by, so she got permission to restore it if she rented to Navy people. She fixed it up and rented it to some officers. Years later, when I was fourteen, she moved into it."

Missy's father bought a beach house when Missy was seven. "My father had polio when he was a child, and he had a horror of one of us getting it. I know he bought that house to get us out of town and avoid polio, although he never said that was the reason. His leg had been affected by polio, but he refused to wear a brace or use crutches. That probably had something to do with the reason he went into orthopaedics."

Missy's family would spend the entire summer at their house on Sullivan's Island. "We'd move over in May and stay until October. For a month before and after summer vacation, we'd drive in to school with my father in the morning. In the fall, people would ask us, 'When are you moving back into the city?' and we'd say, 'After the second hurricane!'

"We were always over there during hurricane season," Missy explains. "Daddy would make sure we had candles and kerosene for the lamps, and we'd listen to the radio until the power went off. It was an old beach house, and sometime it would start leaking.

Once, we had to move the bed to get it from under a leak! My sister and I shared a bedroom with French doors opening to the front porch. When the rain would blow in, we'd put towels on the floor. We just hunkered down and rode it out. It was fun – an adventure! Only once, when I was about ten, somebody came and got us and brought us into the city during a mandatory evacuation when Daddy couldn't come over to get us. But we weren't afraid of hurricanes."

Missy describes their beach house as "a rambling old house but a solid house. It was built up seven feet off the ground. The foundation was tree trunks – they were huge! The original deed said the property went to the high water mark, but when we lived there – and even now - there were two streets of houses built in front of ours."

Missy recalls when the bridge from Mt. Pleasant came onto Sullivan's Island near Ft. Moultrie at "the point – Station 11 or so." She also remembers when the Ben Sawyer Bridge was being constructed. "I learned to water ski with Daddy in what we called the 'borrow pit' where they dug the soil out – they 'borrowed it' - to build the causeway for the new bridge. I'd also go shrimping with him in the creeks behind the island – I'd row the boat and he'd cast the net. And we went crabbing together."

The Sieglings bought their beach house just before the fort closed in 1948, and there was still a movie theater and a skating rink on the island when she was growing up. Missy adds, "My mother would take all the neighborhood kids to the beach - I don't know where she got the nerve to do it! But she was a good swimmer. She grew up swimming in the harbor with her friends, and one time, she participated in a swim from the Ashley to the Cooper River. A couple of her uncles had a sailboat, so she spent a lot of time on the water. It was important to her that we knew how to swim, and she sent us to swimming lessons at the municipal pool on George Street."

When the Sieglings moved to the island for the summer, their black housekeeper went with them. Missy says, "Occasionally, she'd go home on the weekend. But she lived with her daughter and her seven grandchildren in two rooms of a house on Bottle Alley (Jacob's Alley), so I think she liked coming to the island and sleeping in a bed to herself. When we were in town, she came every day Monday through Friday. She was there when we came down for breakfast and stayed until after we'd had our three o'clock dinner. Maids didn't make much money or have much education, but the attitude I understood was that my parents looked after them and tried to help them. Her family would come to Daddy with medical problems, and sometime her grandchildren would come to our house after school and we'd play together. When I was away at college, a friend and I were talking about home, and I said something about our maid. My friend was from Delaware, and they had a maid that came in and cleaned. But they knew absolutely nothing about her. She was just somebody they paid. My friend was amazed that we thought of our maid as part of the family."

Missy remembers that a number of black families lived below Broad Street. They lived on Price's Alley as well as behind the house where she played on lower King Street. And for awhile, her grandmother across the street had black tenants who rented the apartment above her garage.

Missy remembers a black woman would come door-to-door once a week selling vegetables. "She had a basket with vegetables and she carried it on her head." Missy has a pair of watercolor prints by renowned Charleston artist, Elizabeth O'Neill Verner, depicting women carrying a basket of flowers on their heads. She adds, "I remember during the Azalea Festival, the flower ladies would have a competition at The Battery. They'd be singing and dancing while balancing the baskets. I enjoyed watching them."

Missy says, "What I enjoyed most about growing up in Charleston was being so close to everything - and the small town atmosphere. Wherever you went, you knew people. Today, I go to Footlight Plays and I don't know anybody. Everybody has dispersed or moved away. I don't have the feeling of community, other than at church." Missy and her husband are members of Bethel United Methodist Church now that he is retired from the ministry. "I enjoy Bethel and I see people there that I've always known. One woman who is in the choir with me was at Ashley Hall when I was there. But most children of Charleston people don't live here, and as people die, there are fewer and fewer from old families. I think that would be true of any of the churches downtown."

About ten years ago, Missy's family sold her childhood home at 80 Tradd Street. She explains, "There is a lot of upkeep on a wooden single house, and nobody in the family wanted to live there. It was rented out for about twenty years but was hard to rent because it was old and in fragile condition – it was built in 1803." The people who bought it tore down the hyphen – the building that connected the main house to the brick house in the rear where Missy's grandmother had lived. The new owners then divided the property and sold the two houses separately.

A lot of things have changed South of Broad.

THE CHANGING TIMES

Phyllis Dawson Moseley

When asked to name an activity that typifies growing up in Charleston during the 1940s and 50s, Phyllis Dawson Moseley answers, "Dancing and dancing and dancing! There were sock hops in the high school auditorium during recess, and there were sock hops in the gyms after football games. There were the Junior-Senior dances which were wonderful. If you belonged to the Y-Teens, there were formal dances. The girls always got to ask the boys - that was really fun! And I was lucky enough to get on Mrs. Dufour's list for the afternoon tea dances at The Citadel. We also went to Citadel hops – they were great! The bands were something! I even heard Jimmy Dorsey there. There was a receiving line where you shook hands with the president of The Citadel. At that time, it was General Mark Clark. My friends and I had a closet full of evening gowns, so we were always ready for a dance! I always thought we were so lucky.

Phyllis (right) and friends

"Then there was dancing at Seaside and Wurthman's on the Isle of Palms. And the right of passage was the Anchor Lounge – on Meeting Street between the Hibernian and the Courthouse. It was

195

the place to go as you got older. The front had a dance floor and a band and singer. Everybody knew the Anchor! I remember after my high school graduation, my friend's parents took us there, but it wasn't as much fun then as when we went with friends or a date. It was just a great place in the 1950s."

Kate's Drive-in was another popular place. Phyllis describes it: "It was really something. They had a live disk jockey from WTMA sitting up high. We loved to go there and listen to him. If you had a regular date, you'd sit in your car. But if you were going to a dance and were all dressed up, you went inside where they had a restaurant. The Fork was also good. It was an eat-in restaurant, but Daddy would sometimes pick up fried chicken from there and we'd go over to Folly Beach in the evening and have supper on the beach. You could drive right up onto the beach back then."

It seems like everyone loved Labrasca's on the corner of King and Cleveland Streets. "I remember they had a round seat that was covered in satin or velvet. There was an obelisk going up in the middle of it, and people would sit around that. It was a nice place to sit when you had to wait. Another restaurant that really impressed me was Everett's. It was kind of an elegant place. And, if you were lucky when you were older, your date would take you to the Cavallero on Savannah Highway. That was really special."

All of those places are gone now. Phyllis remembers a number of others that have also disappeared. "My daddy owned the Atlantic Grill on Market Street right across from where Charleston Place is now. The father of a friend of ours owned the Star Café on the corner of King and Market. And later, in 1952, Daddy opened the Carriage House on North Market Street. That was in the building that is now T-Bones Restaurant. The Carriage House was a supper club – beautiful. Before that, the Market was a sailor haven, a very shady area. But when Daddy opened the Carriage House, things had changed. There were places like Henry's and bars that were different than the others – classier – that had live music. But my daddy knew nothing about the restaurant business and he lost a lot of money. They eventually also had gambling in the back, but he didn't know anything about that business either. In the late 1950s, Daddy opened the Cove on East Bay Street, and that is where I met my husband."

The area around Market Street is not the only section of the city that has a new identity these days. It was common knowledge, even to the authorities, that West Street was the red light district. There were even policemen stationed on the corner. One building called the Big Brick was notorious for prostitution. "In the past fifteen years or so," Phyllis says, "people have begun living on West Street and making the houses look nice. My husband remarked to his friend a few years ago that the houses on West Street were starting to look good. His friend joked that they always were classy places – they had a sink in every room!

"At one time, the father of my husband's best friend was a pharmacist who had a drug store on King Street near West Street. A lot of his clients were women from that area – prostitutes. But he also filled prescriptions for the nuns from the convent around the corner. So he said his biggest groups of customers were the nuns and the prostitutes and that he lived in dire fear he'd get those orders mixed up one day! Years later, after prostitution left the area, the Big Brick became a bar. I remember one day saying to my father-in-law that we were going there and he said, 'That's operating again?'"

As a child, Phyllis lived uptown at 549 Rutledge Avenue. She says that in the 1940s, Rutledge Avenue was a brick street with the old track from the street car still running down the middle of it. "I remember when they paved it. I didn't understand why because I thought it was so pretty with the bricks. I guess they wanted to pave over the tracks, since the street car was not being used any more."

In her block was her family's church - St. Peter's Episcopal Church - as well as a Baptist church and her grammar school, Mitchell School. "Perry Street runs right between the school and the playground. They would block it off after school so we could roller skate there. The big boys would play street hockey with sticks and tin cans. You had to stay out of their way! Every Christmas, I'd get a new pair of Union #5 skates. Recently, I saw a picture of a skate key on the internet, and under it was the caption, 'Does anybody know what this is?'"

Phyllis says her neighborhood was racially and ethnically mixed and adds, "I think all neighborhoods in the city were. There was a Greek family on one side of us, a black family on the other side, and a number of black people living on the street in back of us. I used to see the Greek children walking to Greek school in the afternoon, and I thought it was sad that they had been in school all day and then had to go again in the afternoon! One time, the Greek girl next door asked me if I wanted a piece of pie. Well, I wasn't going to turn that down - until I heard it was spinach pie! I said, 'No, thank you.' Years later, when I was grown and was working in a doctor's office, the girl's mother came in. I hadn't seen her in years and didn't know what had happened to them, so we were very happy to see each other. Today, there are some Greek people who live in my building, and one of them has an uncle who is married to the girl who offered me the pie! If you talk to Charleston people, you're always going to find some connection."

The black family who lived next to Phyllis had a little girl about her age, too. "She lived with her mother, father, aunt and uncle. The aunt was a schoolteacher. The uncle always dressed real well. The little girl and I got to be friends. We'd yell out for each other to come out and play. Between our yards was a wire fence. We each sat on a stool on our different sides of the fence and played doll babies. We'd make them out of a Pepsi Cola bottle. We'd cut twine for the hair and use a marble and push it into the bottle to hold the twine. We'd braid the twine, put ribbons in it, and pretend they were going to parties.

"One day, the girl said, 'My mother's cooking crabs. I'll go get you one.' It was so good! That was the first time I'd had a crab claw. Another time, my mama and daddy were going out and they asked her mother if she'd babysit. I was about seven. I asked if the little girl could come over, too, and they said yes. We were thrilled to death because it was the first time we were really together face-to-face. We had never played on the street in front together and had only played through the fence. Anyway, we had a big swing on our front porch, and that night we were swinging and having the best time. But her mother came out and said we had to come in because people would think it was not proper. We didn't question it."

Phyllis says she was free to roam and go just about everywhere – except to the playground and to the municipal pool, both of which her father considered to be too rough. "But I could leave my house in the morning and be home for supper. I had friends that lived on other streets and we'd pick them up as we'd go along. That was great! And we'd ride our bikes on the sidewalks. There was a concrete coping around the little patch of grass in front of many houses, and we'd park our bicycles there and pretend it was a parking lot. Even when I was real little, I could ride my tricycle on the sidewalk - and Rutledge was a pretty busy street! We'd ride and take our doll babies to Hampton Park. Later, we would ride to the Girl Scout Hut at Hampton Park for our meetings. We'd also go to the old museum. Nobody seemed to worry about anything."

Sometimes Phyllis would spend the night with her aunt at the Confederate Home on Broad Street. "A lot of elderly ladies lived in apartments there. That was a wonderful place to spend childhood nights! You'd hear St. Michael's Church chimes. It was something special. And we'd go to Robertson's Cafeteria on Broad Street and Coastal Ice Cream Parlor. It was wonderful."

Phyllis says, "Summertime was great! We'd go barefooted everywhere. I'd walk barefooted to my grandmother's on Fishburne Street and have to hop on the grass for awhile because the sidewalk was so hot. I don't know why we didn't wear shoes! The biggest thing I remember about summertime is eating tomato sandwiches on white bread with Duke's mayonnaise."

Phyllis remembers going to summer camp at Seabrook Beach (Camp St. Christopher). "It was like going to the jungle! There were dirt roads and they had to chop places to get cars through there. It was almost scary, or so it seemed to a little girl. We stayed in tin roof cabins. But the beach was fun and the driftwood was unbelievable. And you could find live sand dollars so easily. You'd just rub your feet on the bottom when you were in the ocean. I didn't really like going to camp so much as a kid – the drinking water was awful. But I loved it when I was old enough to be a camp counselor. We didn't have to do much because they had classes for the younger ones – religious, arts and crafts – and there were people that taught those. So the counselors could just lie on the beach and have fun during those sessions. I remember one time there was a hurricane and we had to evacuate the camp. I brought my group to our house in Moreland and we put them up in the attic. The kids thought it was great!"

By that time, Phyllis's family had moved West of the Ashley and she was attending St. Andrew's High School. "St. Andrew's people took tremendous pride in the school. We thought we were smarter and had the best teachers!" But she had loved attending Mitchell Grammar School as well. "I made nice friends and had grand times. Every year, we had the Maypole Festival and had the queen and her court. We also had a play every year. One time, there was a skit of the 'Horace Heidt Show,' a radio program where people would show off their talent – kind of like 'American Idol' today. A man from Charleston had been on the show and had won, so a boy played him in our school play."

Phyllis recalls that, when she was very young during World War II, there was a POW camp West of the Ashley off Colony Drive. "I remember seeing the tents from the highway when I was real little. Recently, my husband's friend bought the chapel and converted it to a home. It is beautiful. He kept some features so that you could see it was originally a chapel. The interesting thing is that when this man was a child, the priest used to take him to this chapel to serve as an altar boy at Mass for the German prisoners - and his father was killed by the Germans in the war."

There are a number of other places in Charleston that have changed since Phyllis's youth. For instance, "The Battery was the place where teenagers used to go to park and smooch. It would be hard to find a parking place there! And you could take boat rides in Colonial Lake."

King Street was always an important landmark. "Everybody did their shopping on King Street. Ladies wore hats and gloves when they went to shop. When my time came, I remember wearing heels and a dress – always! We bought from Elza's, Snelgrove's, Conklin's. My favorite was Rosalie Meyers – I was mostly interested in those evening gowns! One of my favorite things to do was to try on hats in Kerrison's. We usually didn't buy them, but we liked to try them on. A lot of people wore them to church and football games. Anytime you got dressed up, you wore a hat.

"On King Street, between Wentworth and Society Streets, was Hunley's Drugstore. When you were shopping, you stopped in there for an egg salad sandwich and a Coca-Cola. In the summertime, ladies would ask for an 'ammonia Coke.' They had the vapors from the heat, so a drop or two of ammonia was added to the Coca-Cola to revive them. They were drinking ammonia! My mother-in-law said in those days they also used to mix a little kerosene in with sugar and feed it to babies to cut the phlegm! Imagine!"

But Phyllis remembers something else about King Street. "If you were walking on the sidewalk with friends abreast and a black man or woman approached, they'd step off the curb and go around you. Black people couldn't even go to Hampton Park or The Battery unless they had a white child with them that they were taking care of. They had to have a reason to be there."

Phyllis remembers several incidents indicative of the segregated times. "One time, there was a big Girl Scout function and there were some black Girl Scouts there. My father said, 'It's a Communist thing – I know it's Communist!' Another time, after I was grown, a black man came into the doctor's office where I was working and he sat down in the waiting room. The doctor saw him sitting there and said to me, 'Daughter (a common term of endearment), there is a black man sitting in the waiting room. Tell him to go sit in the colored waiting room.' I said, 'I don't think I can do it,' but he said to me, 'You have to do it.' So I did. The black man thanked me and he left. He came back when it was time for his appointment, but after that, there never was a separate black waiting room again. I would love to be able to meet that man today and see if he remembers that and to tell him how, after his visit, we no longer had the separate room. Do you know who that man was? It was (U.S. Congressman) Jim Clyburn."

Years later, there was the hospital strike at MUSC. "Armored tanks were on Rutledge Avenue, on the corner by Ashley Hall School. (Civil rights leader) Ralph Abernathy led the march down Rutledge Avenue and we watched. I was working for a doctor then, and when I left to go home after work, he said, 'Phyllis, you go straight home. Do not go by that Medical University.' But I did drive over there and when I saw the tanks, I turned around. The sun was shining on those bayonets and that scared me so bad I didn't know what to do!"

Phyllis remembers another time, in the early 1960s, there was a young black woman who worked with her. "She was well-liked.

So, one day, several of us from the office were going to go to eat lunch at Raley's Cafeteria on King Street, right next to the Colony Bakery, and we invited her to come with us. She was reluctant but she came. We got a lot of stares."

Things have come a long way since then. And with the many changes Phyllis has witnessed in Charleston over the decades, she mentions another one that has occurred in her own life - Phyllis has discovered that she now likes spinach pie. She can even pronounce it in Greek.

"Spanakopita. And it is delicious!"

ALL AROUND THE TOWN

Sondra Pfaehler

When Sondra Pfaehler was growing up, she lived uptown, downtown and just outside of town. "Uptown, we lived at 160 Grove Street which is two blocks off Rutledge Avenue. When I was ten, we lived downtown with my grandmother at 46 Pinckney Street while we were having our new house built in Moreland, just across the Ashley River."

Her grandmother's downtown area was quite different than Sondra's quiet, idyllic uptown neighborhood of Hampton Terrace. "There were a lot of industrial shops down there in that block of Pinckney. Across the street from my granny's house was an auto shop that my grandfather had owned. I believe he also had the first taxi business in Charleston. Next to Granny's house, Mr. Parham did welding - or something to do with working on cars. His shop faced Church Street and it's now the Andrew Pinckney Inn. On the corner, where the First Baptist School gym is now, there was an ice house. There was a train track, too, and I remember when the train went through there. Another welding shop was two doors up Pinckney from my granny's, on the corner of Maiden Lane. And around the corner on Anson Street, there was a mattress factory."

Although Pinckney Street was comprised primarily of businesses, that's not to say there was nothing for a child to do for fun. "Mr. Ogletree's grocery store was just around the corner on Anson and Hasell Streets. We used to go there all the time. And just up Pinckney, on the corner of Meeting, was Ginsberg's wholesale candy.

"Another thing I remember is the ice man coming around. Granny would let us put the card out on days he was coming. I still remember the cards. They were yellow and black; there was one card that said '5 lbs' and another for '10 lbs.' Granny had an electric refrigerator by the time I came along, but she still had an old icebox on the back porch."

Besides her grandmother's house, there were only a few other residences sprinkled in along the street. "Going up the block, toward Meeting Street, there was a beautiful house where the Indigo Inn's parking lot is now. It was set back off the street. The front of it faced Pinckney Street and the side of it went down Maiden Lane. Going down Pinckney the other way, toward East Bay, there were some wooden Charleston single houses. Black people lived in the two small ones near the corner of Anson Street, and my grandmother's friend lived upstairs in another one. There was also a family she knew living in the house that is now the restaurant (Cru Café) and also the one across from it that is now the vet's office. And there was even a house back on a little alley wedged between my grandmother's house and Mr. Parham's welding shop. But none of those houses had any kids for us to play with, so we just played in the yard mostly."

Sondra's grandparents' house was on a big lot. She says, "When my mother was young, her daddy had built a camper. It had a front like a school bus and a place in the back of it where they could eat and sleep. They'd drive out to Folly Beach and spend the night. Anyway, that old thing was still in the back yard and we played around it."

Sondra's grandmother was born in Charleston and had been a Finnegan. Her grandfather came from Georgetown. He died while he was working at his automotive shop when a car fell on him. Sondra explains, "My mother was only eleven. So she went to work at the Cigar Factory when she was fairly young. Her sister worked at the movie theater, and her other sister worked at the phone company. When I was thirteen or fourteen, my aunt still worked there and got me a summer job there counting switches."

Sondra's father's family, the Pfaehlers, lived uptown on Poplar Street. "They have been in Charleston since the late 1800s - my grandfather was born here. He was the manager of Bulwinkle's Bakery. George Bulwinkle had those famous whipped cream cakes! The bakery was on Rutledge Avenue, right off Cannon Street, where there is a parking lot across from Hominy Grill now. On the corner across the street was Ashley Meat Market. My godfather, Payton Mize, owned it and also Mize Meat Market on the corner of Cannon and President Streets."

Sondra says, "We are German and English and Irish. We went to St. Matthew's and St. Barnabas Lutheran churches as well as Sacred Heart, St. Joseph's and St. Peter's Catholic churches." Sondra has been a member of St. Matthew's Lutheran Church her entire life. She says, "I remember when the choir used to sit on the altar, and I remember being in their candlelight services. But I was confirmed and made First Communion at St. Barnabas. We also went with Mama to the Catholic churches sometimes because she was Catholic. I was in the May Procession at Sacred Heart several times. My cousin and I always ended up sitting together in the front row pew, and we'd get in a fight and they'd have to come take us out!"

Sondra attended James Simons School uptown on King Street. "We walked to school. When I was in fourth grade and we were living with my granny on Pinckney Street, we'd take the city bus to school. My younger sister and I caught the bus from the corner of Meeting and Wentworth and got off uptown at the corner of Moultrie and Rutledge. On the way home, there was a bus stop at Mitchell School, and Miss Cotton, the school nurse there, would get on it and ride back downtown; she would talk to us on the bus.

"I remember that year, after I took my math exam, I left school and caught the bus downtown. When I got to my granny's, it dawned on me that there was another whole blackboard with more math problems that I hadn't even done! My mother called the school and they let me go back and finish it.

"I don't remember a whole lot about elementary school. We used to have recess at the Enston Homes, the old folks' home across the street from the school. There was a big grassy area on the Huger Street side of it, and we would jump rope and play there. Also, I remember we always had the May Pole and had a May Queen and representatives from the different grades. We wore long dresses made of a gauzy material and carried a bouquet of flowers. And I vividly remember Miss Frances Cannon, my first grade teacher."

When she lived on Grove Street, Sondra was fortunate to live just a stone's throw from Hampton Park. "On Sunday, while Mama was cooking dinner, Daddy would take me in my baby carriage to Hampton Park. As we got older, Mama would take us to the zoo there. It was wonderful! The animals were right along the front entrance at Cleveland Street - the birds in the cages, the monkeys, the fenced areas with the buffalo. They may have had some otters or something in pools along in there, too, and the lion was in there somewhere. Farther back were the ducks and the pond. There were pretty wisteria-covered walks back there. And we'd go to the concession stand and get Cracker Jacks. But we mostly played in our back yard." Sondra adds that they would also make 'shoebox trolleys' and have parades along the sidewalk of their quiet oak-lined street.

When they were living uptown, Sondra remembers that her mother would send her to the corner grocery on Rutledge Avenue. "Cohen's Grocery was where Moe's Tavern is now. I used to get in so much trouble because Mama would send me over there for something and I'd spend the change! Mama also used to take us to Botzis Drug Store on the corner of Cleveland Street and Rutledge.

There was another drugstore called Faulkner's on the corner of Grove and King, across from Rivers High School. It had booths where you could sit and order food."

Of course, the premier restaurant uptown was Labrasca's. It was known for Italian food, but they also operated the city's first Chinese restaurant right next door. "The entrance to the Italian restaurant was on King Street, and the entrance to the Chinese Restaurant was on the Cleveland Street side. So you could go in on two different sides. But you could be in either one and order food from the other one. Sometimes, my mother would call them on the phone and order spaghetti for take-out. She'd take them a pot and they'd fill it up and we'd take it home. You could also do that in the Chinese part. Later, when we moved across the bridge, there was a place in Maryville that did that, too."

Sondra remembers when there was a train station on the corner of Grove Street and Rutledge Avenue, where the parking lot for College Park baseball stadium is now. "The train went across the river and out to Walterboro. I remember one time catching it from that station with my grandmother Phaehler, and a lot of soldiers were on the train. Behind it, there was a baseball field where we'd go watch Charleston's minor league baseball team play."

Sondra remembers annual events like the circus and the fair being held over by the Citadel's Hagood Stadium. "And the Christmas parade used to be held during the week – like on a Tuesday eve- ning. We'd go to Granny's house and walk over to King from her house on Pinckney. I also remember my parents talking about the Schutzenfest at the Rifle Club. They didn't have it by the time I came along, but I have pictures of my daddy and grandmother sitting on their car. They'd decorate the cars and they held a parade up there. Also, the men collected points or money or something, and whoever had the most would be king. There were activities all weekend, and on the last night, they'd have a big ball."

Every summer, Sondra's family rented a house for a week or two on Folly Beach. "We stayed in the same house every year. There was a grocery store not far away, and Mama and Daddy would sit at the tables outside there and have coffee. We'd ride the Ferris wheel and the other rides or go to the bowling alley. There was also a boardwalk that had a hot dog place and showers and locker rooms where people could leave their clothes in rented lockers. There used to be bands on the old pier. My mother would talk about when the Dorsey brothers used to play there. There was a crystal ball hanging down from the ceiling where they had the dances. I was too young to go to those, and when I was old enough, they weren't having them anymore."

Sondra with her sister, mother and friends

Sondra remembers taking tap dance lessons with Miss Mamie Forbes at the Dock Street Theater. "And Traynor Ferrillo taught classes in elocution and how to walk gracefully. During Lent, he also produced passion plays at the Gloria Theater. There would be thunder and lightning - the whole thing. We always went to see those."

Sondra's father worked as an auto mechanic and repaired the trucks for C.D. Franke, a food distributer. "I remember him telling us that one time when he was working for them, he was driving over the Old Cooper River Bridge and the brakes went out on the truck when he was coming down the slope into the city! He said he went right across Meeting Street and it finally slowed down to a stop.

"When my daddy left C.D. Franke, he worked for McKeithen Oldsmobile on upper King Street. Then it moved to Calhoun Street, next to the Knights of Columbus. It backed up to Connelly's Funeral Home right around the corner on Meeting Street, and he used to work on their hearses. When he'd come home from work, he had to go out back to the portecochere and leave his clothes out there. Mama used to boil his greasy work clothes in a tub over a fire in the back yard."

Sondra says, in business, "My daddy was an entrepreneur and did a lot of different things. He grew gladiolas on a farm on Johns Island and sold them to Carolina Florist which, at the time, was up on Huger Street behind the Enston Homes. He and Mama would go in the evening on Friday to cut them and bring them on Saturday to the florist. On Saturday, he'd have extra ones and we'd park at the gate to Bethany Cemetery and sell them to people who were visiting the cemetery. My sister and I would play out there. That was a weekend outing for a lot of Charlestonians. They'd all go up there to visit the cemetery and run into people they knew. In later years, once the tradition had ended, my aunt used to carry a water jug in her car so she could water the flowers if she stopped by the cemetery.

"Daddy also owned jukeboxes and pinball machines that were around town. When they'd take the old records out to put new ones in, he sold the records at a shop he rented on upper King Street near the Lincoln Theater. It was a few doors before Spring Street, on the left side of the street. He had wooden tables set up in there and had all size records – 33s, 45s, 78s. I don't even know if his store had a name, and I don't think he even had a cash register - just a cash box. My sister and I worked there selling records every Saturday when I was twelve.

"Daddy also owned two shrimp boats. They'd pull into Adger's Wharf and he paid men to head the shrimp right there. My sister and I would have a table set up with a scale, and when they'd head the shrimp, they would bring their buckets up to the scale and we'd give them twenty-five cents a bucket. That was usually in the evening in the summertime. Daddy owned the boats but didn't go out on them. However, one time, he flew to Campeche, Mexico to meet the boat and he rode back on it with the shrimpers. Later, one of Daddy's boats sank. It was called the *Gypsy*. There's a big painting of it hanging in Henry's Restaurant. Alicia Rhett painted it. We'd go down to Henry's to eat all the time and we'd see it."

Sondra remembers shopping with her mother at the City Market when she was very small. "The sheds in the back were all vegetables. Along the side of the street, you might see men standing around smoking and drinking beer. There were a lot of warehouses and packing sheds. Mr. Parham had a produce shed on North Market Street where the praline shop is now next to T-bones Restaurant."

Although the hucksters (street vendors) came through selling vegetables, Sondra says, "My daddy always had a garden in our back yard uptown. He grew lettuce, carrots, tomatoes, beets and would can vegetables. When we moved West of the Ashley, we had a strawberry patch in our back yard. Daddy would make us work – that German work ethic – and we'd have to weed it. I also learned to cook and my sister did the housework when my mother went to work on weekends for a doctor's answering service in the Francis Marion Hotel."

Sondra's family had a maid who "started coming when I was six months old and worked off and on for my family until my young- est child was born. She came mainly to clean the house - it wasn't full time. She did come quite often, though. Her husband was the chief cook at the Navy hospital and, in the evening, sometime she would go and help him when she left our house. When I was married, she came in the summer and minded my children when I went to work. I remember one time I said, 'Sit down and have a cup of coffee.' She said, 'Oh no. I can't sit at the table with you.' And that was in 1968!"

Sondra remembers that "in 1965, the steeple of St. Matthew's Church caught fire and toppled over. It's still buried in the ground there! If you go through the gate, just to the left of the church, it is cemented into the ground now. They salvaged a lot of wood from it and have made crosses which are sold at the church's tea room in the spring."

The crosses represent a bit of Charleston's history, and Sondra has a number of her grandmother's antiques which are part of her family's history here. She adds, "I've also inherited my granny's love of flowers. I remember seeing her on the porch plucking geraniums. She'd just stick them down in the dirt and they would grow! There is an althea in my yard that came out of her yard."

And she acknowledges, "I carry a jug of water in my car like my aunt did in case I happen to be at the cemetery."

AN IDEAL TIME AND PLACE

Sue Schwerin Veon

"The 1950s were a great time to grow up in Charleston!" says Sue Schwerin Veon. She spent most of those years living with her younger sister and parents at 32 Montagu Street, between Pitt and Smith Streets. She walked almost everywhere – even as a very small child. "All of my friends lived within blocks of each other. On the corner of Rutledge and Montagu was the county library, so we didn't even have to cross any streets except Smith. We spent so much time going there. We also spent a lot of time at the 'old' Charleston Museum, one block up Rutledge from the library. And we'd walk to Moultrie playground by Colonial Lake. We could also walk the other direction to the movies on King Street. I had a wonderful childhood, and it seemed to me that it was a time when nobody worried about anything."

Sue (right) and her sister on Montagu Street

Sue's earliest memories are of family gatherings, since all of her father's family was from Charleston. "I used to like hearing about my

215

father growing up downtown. My father had four brothers, so I had a lot of cousins. We saw a lot of each other," she says. In fact, one of Sue's uncles and his family lived with her grandmother in the apartment upstairs from Sue. The house belonged to her grandmother. "Part of my grandmother's clan had owned the Blacklock House at one point," she adds.

Sue's father worked as a welder at the Charleston Dry Dock - where Dockside (condominiums) is located today. One of her uncles owned Colonial Antique Shop on King Street and lived above it with his wife and kids. Another uncle owned a dry cleaning business uptown near where the Visitor Center and Charleston Music Hall are now. "There were warehouses on John Street. That's how you would approach the back of the laundry. They had a huge door in the back that they'd leave open because it was so hot in there. Next door to the dry cleaners was a Nehi bottling plant. I can remember standing outside watching the bottles on the conveyer belt.

"My mother worked at my uncle's dry cleaners, so we had a maid who was there to clean house and cook dinner and make sure we were okay. But I never remember her calling out to check on us, whereas today every five minutes parents are checking on their kids. Playtime was a very carefree time and it seemed like a carefree place to live. I had the freedom to go places with other kids and everyone was friendly – black and white. You couldn't go too far without someone stopping to talk to you. I remember there was a man who rode a bicycle in our neighborhood, and we'd chase after him because he'd stop and give us bubble gum and tell us stories. I couldn't tell you a story he told, but you sure wouldn't do that nowadays!"

Sue says her childhood wasn't very exciting but it seemed there was always something going on. "We used to have shoebox trolley parades around Colonial Lake. I remember decorating shoeboxes with cut-out windows. We'd put a lit candle in it and pull the trolley along with a string.

"We didn't have any particular place to go or things to do. I'd just say, 'Mama, can I go to Kathy's?' and she'd say sure – no questions asked. I don't know if boys had the same freedom. But I never went beyond where they would've wanted me to go anyway, since all my friends were nearby. We played kickball at the horse lot and softball at Moultrie playground. We used to pack lunches on Saturday and go down to the playground and hang out at 'the dump' where they were filling in the marsh. We'd feed the birds."

Sue attended parochial school at the Cathedral of St. John the Baptist. Her mother would drive them to school on her way to work, and Sue and her sister would walk home. "I thoroughly enjoyed my time at Cathedral. I was there from kindergarten through the 8th grade." She laughs when she remembers that "a lady who lived next door to the school used to sell us hot dogs through the fence at lunchtime a couple of times a week. That was our hot lunch! You were dying to be the first one out there to get in line to buy it!" She also smiles when she says the Carter-May Home was behind the school. "Can you imagine - the old folks' home was in the recess yard of the school! All of that is gone now."

Sue says, "We went to church at St. Mary's on Hasell Street but I made my First Communion and Confirmation at Cathedral because I went to school there. The nuns made the communion wafers in the basement of the convent on Legare Street. Part of our instruction for First Communion was to go over there and help make them."

Sue attended high school at Bishop England on Calhoun Street. There were kids from all over – they weren't just from the city – but we still stuck in our little group from Cathedral. We had such a close-knit group of kids, and it just felt familiar, since there were over a hundred in our high school class. We recently had our 50th class reunion.

There is a small group – eight or so girls – that I still have lunch with. They are mostly Cathedral kids but there are some other Bishop England girls, too. Three of us went the whole way from kindergarten to 8th grade together. The rest in our group are from the other downtown Catholic schools – Sacred Heart, St. Patrick's and St. Joseph's. These are the girls I hung out with in high school, probably because I knew some of them from the ball fields we'd played on together when we were younger. It was funny that the kids from these other downtown teams ended up at Bishop England with us. They had always been our opponents on sports teams but then we were supposed to become friends in high school!"

Sue adds, "I didn't even know many kids from the suburbs. Kids from the suburbs had to catch a bus home, so many of them didn't get to join clubs. I could stay as late as I wanted at school for clubs because I could walk home. For us to go West of the Ashley was like going to another city. We would go to a restaurant or a drive-in movie. We used to go to the Magnolia Drive-in movie theater on Savannah Highway. The North 52 (on Rivers Avenue) was another one. We could get a driver's permit at 14. A right of passage was to drive over the old Cooper River Bridge with your mother or father in the car before you'd be allowed to do it with other kids in the car. One of my friends had an uncle with a convertible Cadillac. On the weekend, he'd let her drive it and we'd go to the beach at Sullivan's Island for the day.

"When we got our license, we'd head over to the Holly House. That was our hangout - it was right over the Ashley River Bridge. I was in high school before I remember going to a nice restaurant. We hardly ever ate out – most people didn't. If we did, we'd usually just pick up fried chicken, hamburgers and onion rings from Kate's Drive-In or The Fork and take it home. And there was Pete's Hot Dogs - with chili on them - across from the Piggly Wiggly uptown on Meeting Street. The only place we 'ate in' was at Labrasca's."

Sue explains, "You didn't get anything fancy if you ate out. I remember eating at the restaurant at the Charleston Inn once – where the Marriott is now near the City Marina on Lockwood - and getting a baked potato. I'd never had one before! At home, we always had rice and gravy with our meat! Then they asked me if I wanted sour cream on it and I thought, 'No, why would I want that?' I also never ate a salad until I was older. At home, we'd have sliced tomatoes with a drop of mayonnaise on it. That was your salad. Or my aunt would fix sliced pineapple with a little mayonnaise and a bit of cheddar cheese on it."

There may have been very few restaurants in the city, but there were plenty of stores on King Street. "I have a phone book from 1948 and looked through it to help me think of some of the stores. There was Legerton's (which later became Hugueley's) on the corner of Wentworth. Also, the Fashion Center, Annette's Blue Gown, The Bandbox, Anne's, Davidson's, Diana. Mary Hawkins had a dress shop next to St. Mary's Church on Hasell Street. We'd always go to Condon's and see Santa or the Easter Bunny who would be walking around the store giving out candy. There were also bakeries like the Federal Bakery. Every year Mama would buy my birthday cake from Taylor's on King. According to their ad in the old phone book, they also sold Jewish bakery products.

"Our maid would take us to the movies on King Street when we were younger. I remember going to the Riviera and Gloria and going through a side entrance and up the stairs to sit in the mezzanine or balcony, we called it. We loved going with her because we liked sitting up there, but she had to sit up there because she was black. When my mother or father would take her home in the evening, she would sit in the back seat, even if nobody else was in the car. She lived uptown in an all-black neighborhood." Although many neighborhoods in the city were mixed racially, Sue says, "I don't remember any black people living on our street. However, there were some black families living on Bull Street behind where we lived and also a small black church there."

Sue was out of school when integration began in Charleston in 1963 and remembers that it was mainly peaceable. Later, during the hospital workers strike at MUSC, she says, "I was working at St. Francis Hospital and there were people giving out fliers. Even though St. Francis wasn't part of the strike, we were told not to take the fliers."

Before going to work at St. Francis, Sue had studied there to be a nurse. "The building is still there near the corner of Ashley Avenue, but it's now part of MUSC. It was a really good program. It was the equivalent of a four-year program but was done in three years because you went year-round. One of the things that interested me most about St. Francis Nursing School was that I'd heard from my cousin that seniors did a pediatric rotation in Washington, DC. But wouldn't you know it - the year I started, they changed and we did the pediatric rotation at the Medical College next door!

"All the nursing students at lived at the school. The third, fourth and fifth floors were dorms and the top floor was where the nuns lived. Some of them taught us; others were nurses at the hospital. But you never knew they were up there unless you saw them on the elevator – they never came to our floors. The second floor was where the classrooms were, and the first floor had the headmistress's office and a big lounge area. We could date but we had strict curfews. A house mother sat on the first floor in the evening. She was a little old lady who would ask the boy for his name and then call upstairs and tell us that our date was there."

Sue explains that the nursing students were the work force at the hospital. "There were twenty-eight girls in my class. We were in school half the time and worked at the hospital half the time. We put in a certain amount of hours per week as staff, so they counted on us being there. I remember one time in the summer, I went to the beach and got sunburned. I was supposed to work the next day, and the nun on duty at the hospital came over and got me out of the bed. She said sunburn was no excuse."

Sue graduated in 1965 and the nursing program was ended a few years later. "I was sad when it closed," Sue says. "The school had been around nearly seventy years. We have an annual party in the summer at the island house of one of the alumnae, and we have a Christmas party the first Wednesday in December. It is a reunion of all the classes who went there. We have people with walkers and in wheelchairs as well as others closer to my age."

Sue worked as a nurse at St. Francis when it was still downtown, but she acknowledges, "I wanted to live in the suburbs once I had my own family. I didn't like old things - a house with old windows or paint this thick. I also liked the idea of having a big backyard and owning my home. Most people in the city didn't own their homes. My parents rented their entire lives. Many people moved to the suburbs for the same reasons I did."

The downtown Charleston where Sue grew up has changed. The convent on Legare Street where she helped the nuns make communion wafers is gone. Her uncle's dry cleaners is gone. "We used to go to Oakman's Drug Store on the corner of Rutledge and Calhoun. I think there is a doctor's office there now. And I remember taking dancing lessons at a big hotel on the corner of Hasell and Meeting – the Charleston Hotel. It had a huge staircase inside. It's gone. The only old hotels left are the Francis Marion and the Fort Sumter Hotel which is now condos. My sister had her wedding reception there. I remember it was really nice.

"But all three places my family lived are still there - our first house on Darlington Avenue and our last apartment on Vanderhorst Street, and the house on Montagu where we lived the longest. Yet it has all changed. When you think of all the money people today have put into those old houses! Most of the stores where I shopped are still there, but with different names these days.

"But something I really miss is the smell of food coming from people's houses. I'll be out walking in my neighborhood and I can smell someone fixing pot roast. It will remind me of growing up downtown. You just don't smell food anymore. Nobody's cooking, or if they are, the windows aren't open so you don't have the aroma filtering out."

These days, those enticing aromas are likely to be emanating from a world-class restaurant.

A BLAST FROM THE PAST
Martin Lazarus

Take a ride on Upper King Street today and you'll find a picturesque assortment of storefronts harkening back to the mid-19th and 20th centuries, facades that make us feel as though we are stepping into a movie set. In fact, the area has actually been used as a movie set a time or two. But Martin Lazarus can tell you first-hand about the area when he was growing up during the 1940 and 50s.

"My father was a pharmacist at the Service Cut-Rate Drug Store on King Street, the biggest independent drug store in the city at the time. It was in the building that later became the Old Home Furniture (Sonny Goldberg) store. When it went out of business, my father opened a small drugstore by the same name right next door, at 451 King, across from the American Theater."

Martin's father had his own drug store for ten years. "When he bought it, he carried over some clientele from the previous owner, but then they all left the city or died off. By the mid-1960s, the area had become a less-travelled part of King Street, so we closed. My father then went to work at Henry's Drug Store which was a little farther up on King, near Morris Street."

In Martin's youth, the Upper King Street area was a thriving retail district, and many of the businesses were owned by Jewish proprietors. Metropolitan Clothing and Furniture was owned by Martin's cousin, Max Kirshtein. (Their legendary television ads featured employee Clarence-don't-turn-nobody-down-McCants.) Livingstain's was across from his father's drug store. They sold light fixtures. Robinson's bicycle shop, on the corner of Ann Street, is where Martin got his first bicycle and first baseball glove. (There is a restaurant there now, but the bicycle is still on top of the sign.) And Sonny Goldberg's former store even has a plaque on the wall remembering its owner, the famous "King Street Singer," known for his amusing television commercials. Sonny's father's store, J.L. Goldberg, was across from it and is now a store that sells eclectic home furnishings. Mendelson's Clothing now houses a hair salon, and Chase Furniture is now part of the Charleston School of Law. Bluestein's, Jacob and Son's, and Edward's were a little farther up. "Edward's Five and Dime on the corner of Morris Street was owned by the Kronsbergs who were founding members of our synagogue (Emanu-El), the Conservative synagogue. The Kronsbergs were very generous people, very philanthropic. There is a big portrait of Mr. Ed Kronsberg hanging in Roper Hospital, and a wing of the hospital is named for him."

Martin was born in 1944 at the Catholic hospital, old St. Francis, on Calhoun Street. "Most of the Jewish babies in my age group were born there. Dr. Steinberg delivered me. He was our doctor as we grew up also. His office was on Rutledge Avenue, near Smith Street, but he also made house calls."

Martin explains, "I spent the first few years of my childhood living at 57-B Peachtree Street, a duplex in the area behind The Citadel and Hampton Park. The house is still there. We rented. Most people did." His father rode a bicycle to work. But when his father had a heart attack at the age of forty-one, Martin's mother had to get a job. "She went to work at the newspaper. We didn't have much at that time. We moved to 171-B Gordon Street, another street in the same neighborhood. It was a duplex owned by the Altman furniture people. Israel Altman owned that whole block of houses. Then we moved to the Shore View Apartments on Amelia Street – across from where the old WUSN radio station was. That area is now filled with expensive new homes and condos and is called Longborough."

Martin attended James Simons School for grades 1-7. "I started 8th grade at Rivers High School, but my family moved across the Ashley to South Windermere before the year was over, so I went to St. Andrew's High School for the second half of the 8th grade and for the next four years. I graduated from St. Andrew's. It was a lot harder school than Rivers had been, and I didn't like that I was separated from kids I grew up with. Today, I'd rather go to the 50th reunion of Rivers than to the one for St. Andrew's because I don't feel as close to them as I did to the Rivers and Simons kids."

Martin says most of his life until age thirteen centered around the synagogue. "Synagogue Emanu-El was right in my own neighborhood – on Gordon Street. So all my friends were right there. And there were always a lot of bar mitzvah parties because there were so many of us. My cousin and I had a double bar mitzvah in September 1957. It was the first of its kind in Charleston, since it's usually a solo event.

Martin (right) and his cousin at their Bar Mitzvah

"A good many Jewish kids attended James Simons School. For important Jewish holidays, the school would be nearly empty because so many Jewish kids were absent. But my neighborhood was a mixture of Jewish and Christian families. I had a good friend who was Greek. We all played football together in front of the synagogue. I also played baseball on a little league team sponsored by the Jewish Community Center. We played other teams sponsored by various businesses around the city. Our games were at Moultrie Playground and Hampton Park Playground. In 1955 or '56, our team won the city championship and the trophy is on display at the JCC. I had a baseball that we'd used, and I donated it to them to go with it."

At the time, the Jewish Community Center was on St. Philip Street - between Calhoun and George Streets, where the College of Charleston's Simmons Center for the Arts is now. An Orthodox synagogue, Brith Sholom, stood right next to it. That synagogue later moved to Rutledge Avenue and the JCC moved West of the Ashley. "Our congregation also moved to a new building west of the Ashley, and the property of our original synagogue on Gordon Street was sold to a black congregation which still owns it."

When Martin was growing up, "Jewish kids hung around mostly with Jewish kids. When I was a kid, on Saturdays my friends and I would walk to the movies or do something together after services at the synagogue. I was president of the junior congregation at our synagogue. On Sunday, we had Hebrew school in the morning and then usually had youth activities at the JCC in the afternoon. At age twelve, we'd have additional classes several afternoons a week, after regular school, to prepare for bar mitzvah.

"Back in that day, Jewish people must've decided that they were all going to have babies at the same time because there were ten or twelve families just in our neighborhood that had kids between 1941 and 1944. Not all of my friends belonged to the same synagogue that I did, but we were all members of the Junior Boosters and the AZA (youth organization). Kids from all three synagogues came. There were dances, and we had kings and queens for the dances."

In addition to youth activities, Martin worked in his father's drug store when he was a teenager. "We had delivery boys on bikes, but I'd usually run errands in the car - like going to Geer Drug on East Bay Street (in front of where Harris Teeter is now) to pick up special medicines and supplies. My parents, my older brother and I all worked until 8 or 9 o'clock at night. When we were working, my father and brother and I would go home to eat our big meal in the middle of the day while my mother stayed in the store. We had a maid who cooked and cleaned. She cooked us typical Southern food - fried chicken, calves' liver, tongue, salmon croquets. But the red rice – my mother made that." Martin says it was a specialty of hers, even though she was not a native Charlestonian. "My father was born here but my mother was from New York. Her biggest complaint about living in Charleston was the giant cockroaches!"

Martin explains, "We couldn't afford to keep a kosher household – it's pretty expensive. But my grandmother was strict Orthodox. I can remember going over to her house on Maple Street and turning off her electricity for the Sabbath. She was my mother's mother and moved down here from New York at some point after I was born. She taught me how to play cards. I have fond memories of her. Daddy's parents came from Russia and had also settled in New York briefly before moving to Charleston. When they came here, my grandfather opened his own shoe repair shop on King Street which he later moved to Summerville."

Like many Charlestonians, Martin smiles remembering the day when he could ride the Rutledge-Grove bus to the movies, get a candy bar or popcorn, ride the bus back home, and still have a dime left from the fifty cents he'd started with. He frequented the Riviera, the Arcade, the Garden, and the Gloria Theaters. "Stars were in the ceiling there. We loved it! And upstairs from the Gloria Theater, there was the M&M bowling alley. You'd go up from an entrance near George Street. One time when I was there, a man on the alley next to mine put his arm back to throw his ball just as

I was walking by. He was on the edge of his alley and brought the ball straight back and knocked out my two front teeth! My lip was swollen up to my nose. Dr. Feldman sewed up my gums."

As a young boy, another recreational past-time for Martin was bike riding - "mostly just to have something to do. I went all over the city, even as far as Colonial Lake." But there were a few specific events he recalls from his childhood. "Once a year, a representative from Hatacol Vitamins would come to the American Theater and put on a special program geared toward kids." There would be prizes and other enticements.

Another memory he has is when Hurricane Gracie hit in 1959. "The electricity went out and my father was giving away the ice cream from the store. All of it was going to melt anyway. A lot of people were complaining when somebody else got an ice cream sandwich and all they got was a popsicle!"

As teenagers, Martin and his friends used to get together at each others' houses and play cards – poker and gin – or listen to music and dance. "But sometimes we would go to the Holly House just across the Ashley River Bridge or Piggy Park on Rutledge Avenue or to the Patio on Spring Street. And we went to The Pizzeria – across from Rivers High School - the best pizza in the whole wide world! That's where I first ate pizza. The Pizzeria was in a basement. Can you imagine a house in Charleston with a basement! We also used to go to Big John's Tavern on East Bay Street near Market Street. They had nickel pinball and beer and boiled shrimp." Martin says occasionally they'd go to College Park on the corner of Rutledge Avenue and Cleveland Street to see Charleston's minor league baseball team play. They were called the 'Charleston Rebels' and were owned by Bill Ackerman, a prominent lawyer in town.

But Martin acknowledges his family seldom left the peninsula when he was a child. "We never came across the Ashley River

Bridge except to visit my cousins and aunt and uncle in Byrnes Down. That was about the most we travelled. I never went to James Island or North Charleston. When I moved back to Charleston after living away for more than a decade during and after college, I didn't know my way around those areas."

Martin found himself on Upper King Street not long ago and had a flashback. "My wife and I went to a show at the Charleston Music Hall on John Street and wanted to get something to eat afterward. We went into a pizza place around the corner in the old Service Cut-Rate Drug Store building on King Street! I was showing her, 'That's where the ten-cent coke machine was. That's where the ice cream cooler was, where the magazine rack was, where the pharmacy was.' I hadn't been in there in forty-five years!

"It was very nostalgic."

AFTERWORD

In decades to come, local residents will undoubtedly have their own stories to tell about what made Charleston special in this century. The memory of Charleston for these folks will not mirror the stories you've read in this book, but theirs will still be a memory worth sharing. It is likely to include the wonderful restaurants, the beautifully restored homes, the annual festivals, the amazing golf courses, the world-class hotels and the island resorts. These attributes make Charleston alluring to people who have come seeking a different world from the ones they left. Today's real estate investors, patrons of the arts, college students and retired snowbirds are among the new inhabitants. These newcomers will leave their mark on things, just as the second half of the 20th Century brought about a sea-change through suburban migration, the expansion of the Navy Yard, and the advent of tourism. The Charleston of today will be talked about in years to come, just as the Charleston of the past has been chronicled in these pages, because there is one constant: Charleston has always been, and will always be, unique.

ABOUT THE AUTHOR

Mary C. Coy is a fourth-generation Charlestonian. A 1975 graduate of 'old' Bishop England High School, she holds a BS and M.Ed. from the College of Charleston and is a former educator in local classrooms, museums and historic sites. She is a registered city tour guide, lecturer and free-lance writer for local publications and is the author of a number of books about Charleston, including *The Civil War Walking History Book; The Revolutionary War Walking History Book; Uptown Whirl; Charleston: From a Kid's-Eye View;* and *Charleston 101* (which is also available as an audio book CD narrated by Charlestonians in their 'native tongue').

Made in the USA
Columbia, SC
31 May 2021

38509251R00137